ASIAN POLITICAL, ECONOMIC AND SECURITY ISSUES

SOUTH KOREA

ECONOMIC, POLITICAL AND SOCIAL ISSUES

Asian Political, Economic and Security Issues

Additional books in this series can be found on Nova's website under the Series tab.

Additional E-books in this series can be found on Nova's website under the E-books tab.

Global Political Studies

Additional books in this series can be found on Nova's website under the Series tab.

Additional E-books in this series can be found on Nova's website under the E-books tab.

ASIAN POLITICAL, ECONOMIC AND SECURITY ISSUES

SOUTH KOREA

ECONOMIC, POLITICAL AND SOCIAL ISSUES

ABEL L. HINES
AND
DARRIN O. MULLINS
EDITORS

Nova Science Publishers, Inc.
New York

For permission to use material from this book please contact us:
Telephone 631-231-7269; Fax 631-231-8175
Web Site: http://www.novapublishers.com

LIBRARY OF CONGRESS CATALOGING-IN-PUBLICATION DATA

South Korea : economic, political, and social issues / editors, Abel L. Hines and Darrin O. Mullins.
p. cm.
Includes index.
ISBN 978-1-61942-377-0 (hardcover)
1. Korea (South)--Economic conditions--1988- 2. Korea (South)--Economic policy--1988- 3. Korea (South)--Politics and government--2002- 4. Korea (South)--Social conditions--1988- I. Hines, Abel L. II. Mullins, Darrin O.
HC467.96.S684 2011
330.95195--dc23
2011046191

Published by Nova Science Publishers, Inc. † New York

CONTENTS

PREFACE

In this book, the authors have gathered and present topical research in the study of the economic, political and social issues facing South Korea today. Topics discussed include the adoption of information and communication technology (ICT) in South Korea; labor market policy on non-regular employment in South Korea; the elderly population and South Korea's demographic dilemma; U.S.-South Korea relations and the role, purpose, and results of the Kaesong Industrial Complex (KIC).

Chapter 1 - In this paper, the authors will attempt to find whether there exist any differences in adopting and diffusing information and communication technology (ICT) among developing, newly developed and developed countries. The main research question is to find the factors that play a key role in adopting and diffusing ICT among these countries. To answer this research question, the authors adopted the Unified Theory of Acceptance and Use of Technology (UTAUT) that consists of effort expectancy, performance expectancy and social influence and innovation diffusion functions. This study investigates how the three factors in the United Theory of Acceptance and Use of Technology affect the adoption in the three innovation diffusion phases. The cellular phone was chosen to represent ICT as it is considered to be the most prevalently used and rapidly evolving ICT. Thailand, South Korea, and the U.S. represent the developing, newly developed and developed countries, respectively. Cellular phone adopters in Thailand, South Korea, and the U.S. were surveyed for their experiences. To analyze the data, the survival analysis was used because it can explain the characteristics of the potential adopters or non-adopters. The ICT diffusion patterns, as well as the ICT diffusion factors, of the three countries are found to be different. The authors also believe that the results of this study can be utilized to build a strategy in reducing the digital divide gaps among countries.

Chapter 2 - The demographic composition of any nation's populace is in constant flux, with new challenges arising along with demographic shifts. Few nations, however, face as serious a quandary as does South Korea at the dawn of the 21st century. The South Korean populace is rapidly becoming disproportionately elderly, with far too few births occurring each year to maintain a solidly youthful population base. To provide an illustrative description of the problematic shift, consider some basic geometric shapes. First, imagine a robust population as a pyramid-shaped beaker with a broad base that decreases in circumference as the beaker ascends in height. At the base, the broadest area of the beaker, are the youngest members of the populace, with the working age demographic immediately above them and—owing to the forces of nature (e.g., disease and congenital health issues) and the ordinary dangers that accompany modern life (e.g., automobile accidents, fires, homicides, and workplace fatalities)—the size of the working age demographic slowly contracts as does the authors hypothetical pyramid-shaped population beaker as it ascends. At the top, the point at which the perimeter of the beaker is most constricted, are the elderly.

Chapter 3 - Since late 2008, relations between the United States and South Korea (known officially as the Republic of Korea, or ROK) have been arguably at their best state in decades. By the middle of 2010, in the view of many in the Obama Administration, South Korea had emerged as the United States' closest ally in East Asia.

Chapter 4 - This purpose of this report is to provide an overview of the role, purposes, and results of the Kaesong Industrial Complex (KIC) and examine U.S. interests, policy issues, options, and legislation. The KIC is a six-year-old industrial park located in the Democratic People's Republic of Korea (DPRK or North Korea) just across the demilitarized zone from South Korea. As of the end of 2010, over 120 medium-sized South Korean companies were employing over 47,000 North Korean workers to manufacture products in Kaesong. The facility, which in 2010 produced \$323 million in output, has the land and infrastructure to house two to three times as many firms and workers. Products vary widely, and include clothing and textiles (71 firms), kitchen utensils (4 firms), auto parts (4 firms), semiconductor parts (2 firms), and toner cartridges (1 firm).

In: South Korea ISBN: 978-1-61942-377-0
Editors: A. L. Hines and D. O. Mullins

Chapter 1

THE GAP IN ADOPTING ICT AMONG DEVELOPING, NEWLY DEVELOPED, AND DEVELOPED COUNTRIES: IN THE CASE OF THAILAND, SOUTH KOREA AND THE US

Kyung Hoon Yang[1,*], Sang Gun Lee[2] and Jae Kyung Kim[3]

[1]Department of Management Information Systems,
School of Business Administration, University of Wisconsin, US
[2]Department of Management,
College of Business Administration, Ajou University, South Korea
[3]Department of Management, Marketing, and Information Systems
State University of New York College at Oneonta, US

ABSTRACT

In this paper, the authors will attempt to find whether there exist any differences in adopting and diffusing information and communication technology (ICT) among developing, newly developed and developed countries. The main research question is to find the factors that play a key role in adopting and diffusing ICT among these countries. To answer this research question, the authors adopted the Unified Theory of Acceptance and Use of Technology (UTAUT) that consists of effort expectancy,

---

* Email: yanguwlax.edu.

performance expectancy and social influence and innovation diffusion functions. This study investigates how the three factors in the United Theory of Acceptance and Use of Technology affect the adoption in the three innovation diffusion phases.

The cellular phone was chosen to represent ICT as it is considered to be the most prevalently used and rapidly evolving ICT. Thailand, South Korea, and the U.S. represent the developing, newly developed and developed countries, respectively. Cellular phone adopters in Thailand, South Korea, and the U.S. were surveyed for their experiences. To analyze the data, the survival analysis was used because it can explain the characteristics of the potential adopters or non-adopters. The ICT diffusion patterns, as well as the ICT diffusion factors, of the three countries are found to be different. The authors also believe that the results of this study can be utilized to build a strategy in reducing the digital divide gaps among countries.

Keywords: Innovation Diffusion, Technology Acceptance, Digital Divide

1. Introduction

Information and communication technology (ICT) is considered an enabler of ‘the third wave’ that could change the status and wealth of nations. It is generally believed that the digital divide between developed and developing countries would be reduced while opposite directions of the ICT effect would enlarge the gap of digital divide.

In this study, the authors investigate whether the attitudes and perceptions of ICT adopters of developing countries are different from those of newly developed or developed countries, whether such differences delay the adoption of new ICT, and what critical factors play key roles in adopting new ICT among countries. In order to answer the above questions, the authors first compared the time series data of ICT adoption to analyze the pattern of the ICT adoption. Then, the authors studied the factors that differentiate the ICT adoption patterns. The authors used the Unified Theory of Acceptance and the Use of Technology (UTAUT) model consisting of the effort expectancy, performance expectancy and the social influences based upon previous research in the field (Venkatesh et al., 2003). Third, the authors identified a group of people who frequently changed their cellular phones and service companies, and investigated their roles in cellular phone diffusion among the countries. The authors postulated there are two types of cellular phone adopters: early adopters and the frequent changers of cellular phones or service companies. The former adopt new ICT sooner, while the later lead the continuous diffusion of ICT.

The three countries, Thailand, South Korea, and the U.S were selected to represent a developing, newly developed, and developed country. The authors also chose cellular phones as the ICT, because they are popularly used in all three countries, and the adoption of the cellular phone is decided by the individual. We surveyed the cellular phone adopters in Thailand, South Korea, and the U.S. for 15 years from 1989 to 2003 (the initial data collection points vary among the countries). The results can be used to build a strategy to reduce the digital divide gap of countries.

2. Literature Review

2.1. Adoption and Diffusion of Technology Innovation

Since Ryan and Gross (1943) discussed the diffusion of technology innovation, this has been a fascinating research topic that has spilled over to other academic fields including information systems studies. In the discipline of management information systems, Rogers (1995) raised this issue with his diffusion of innovations (DOI) theory and many researchers suggested several theories, frameworks, and research methods such as the technology acceptance model (TAM) (Davis, 1989), theory of planned behavior (Taylor and Todd, 1955), and social cognitive theory (Compeau and Higgins, 1995). As research evolves, the main topics of research have focused on the patterns and extent of ICT diffusion and the propensity of an adopter to adopt and assimilate ICT (Fichman, 2000). While these theories have played a profound role in developing this field, they do not apply equally well to all types of ICT innovation in all adoption contexts (Fichman, 2000).

At the initial stage of research, researchers focused primarily on developing theories about the adoption of innovations by individuals (Agarwal, 2000). Later, individual-level ICT adoption and diffusion studies expanded to the organizational-level that includes all unit levels within an organization as research found that the critical factors for ICT adoption and diffusion for individuals were completely different from those for organizations. For example, Gallivan (2001) pointed out that these traditional individual level innovation adoption frameworks may not fit well when used in more complex technologies and adoption scenarios, which require high levels of coordination across multiple adopters or where the technology has a high knowledge burden.

TAM and DOI theory models are applied to situations where the individual user can voluntarily decide their adoption of the ICT. DOI theory identifies five perceived attributes of an innovation as influencing the adoption behavior: relative advantage, complexity, compatibility, trialability, and observability.

In contrast, TAM was created specifically to explain IT adoption, and it posits just two perceived attributes that influence adoption: usefulness and ease-of-use. Burkhardt and Brass (1990) researched adopter centrality in the communication network. Their findings showed that the earlier adopters were centrally located in the network, the less change occurred in the power structure.

Different types of ICT were studied to shed light on the adoption and diffusion phenomenon. Swanson (1994) classified ICT into three types. Type I innovation is an IS process innovation. There are two sub-types of Type I: Type I(a) is an IS administrative process innovation, such as IS outsourcing, and Type I(b) is an IS technological process innovation, such as computer-assisted systems engineering (CASE) tools, database management systems (DBMS), and object-oriented processing systems (OOPS).

Type II innovation is an IS product and business administrative process innovation, such as the information center, executive information systems (EIS), payroll, personnel record systems, accounting information systems (AIS), teleconferencing, expert systems (ES), e-mail, etc.

Type III innovation involves inter-organizational IS innovation and has three sub-types. Type III (a) is an IS product and business technological process innovation, such as material requirements planning (MRP) and computer integrated manufacturing (CIM). Type III (b) is an IS product and business product innovation, such as airline reservation systems.

Type III (c) includes IS product and business integration innovation, such as electronic data interchange (EDI). Swanson's framework was verified by Grover et al. (1997).

Based on Swanson's model, Prescott and Conger (1995) classified ICT into an IS unit locus of impact such as CASE tools and DBMS; intra-organization locus of impact, such as the Distributed DBMS document imaging system, spreadsheets, joint application design (JAD), and information center; and inter-organization locus of impact, such as the EDI. For each type, they did a factor research (individual level and organizational level) and stage research (longitudinal, repeated measure).

2.2. United Theory of Acceptance and Use of Technology

Previous researchers found that a framework of the individual level or organization level alone does not fit and cannot explain the symptom well. Hence, they found it necessary to combine the individual level and organization level. Furthermore, as Swanson (1994) said, the adoption attitude and strategy is different according to the type of ICT, and the ICT itself should be considered. Venkatesh et al. (2003) suggested the United Theory of Acceptance and Use of Technology (UTAUT), which combined the most widely-used eight ICT adoption models. These adoption models are the theory of reasoned action, the technology acceptance model, the motivational model, the theory of planned behavior, a model combing the technology acceptance model and the theory of planned behavior, the model of PC utilization, the innovation diffusion theory, and the social cognitive theory. The model consists of performance expectancy, effort expectancy, social influence and facilitating conditions. Performance expectancy is defined as the degree to which an individual believes that using the system will help him or her to attain gain in their job performance. Effort expectancy is defined as the degree of ease associated with the use of the system. Social influence is defined as the degree to which an individual perceives it important others believe he or she should use the new system. Facilitating conditions are defined as the degree to which an individual believes that an organizational and technical infrastructure exists to support use of the system. However, facilitating conditions do not apply when analyzing the countries because of their different cultures. Therefore we deleted the factor from our research model.

3. Research Model and Hypotheses

3.1. Model Perspectives

Our purpose is to analyze the ICT adoption of developing countries in comparison with other newly developed and developed countries. A model that demonstrates and compares the ICT adoption pattern of countries should consider economic, political, cultural, geographic, demographic, technology infrastructure, and the adopters' behavioral factors. Economic factors, such as the price of cellular phones, disposable income, consumer behavior, and economic situation, determine the adoption of ICT. The main factor involving the political environments of ICT adoption would be the government regulation. Depending on the regulation, ICT adoption will be different. Cultural factors, for example, allowing the use of ICT in certain places, can affect adoption. The technology infrastructure also affects ICT adoption, as well as geography and demographic, such as population or the size of a nation. However, the attitude of adopters is considered the most important factor in ICT adoption and we focused on adopter attitudes in our research.South Korea represents a newly developed country for its economic development and advancement in ICT. For the developed country, we considered the U.S. and Finland. Finland is advanced in the cellular phone industry and the U.S. is the icon for developed countries. We then chose the U.S. because of its economic, cultural, political influences over other countries. For the developing country, several countries in Africa, Asia, and South America were considered, but Thailand was ultimately chosen because of its economic and technological aspects as well as the ease of access for data collection. Located in the center of Southeast Asia, Thailand has made impressive economic advancements over the past few decades. Its average annual economic growth was about 8 percent between 1976 and 1996. Between 1988 and 1996, the number of people living in poverty was reduced by more than half, falling from 32 to 11 percent. This progress came to a sudden halt in 1997 when the Asian financial crisis hit. This crisis had a severe impact on the Thailand economy. The Gross Domestic Product (GDP) dropped by over 10 percent in 1998, and the GDP per capita dropped back to its 1994 levels. The economy started to recover in 1999. We choose the cellular phone as a sample of ICT. At the beginning, we considered the cellular phone, MP3, telematics, LAN, database software, MS Windows, and ERP. However, we selected the cellular phone, because it is an individual-based ICT and is used the most. Figure 1 shows general information for the three countries.

3.2. Research Model

The research model of this research consists of three parts. The first part is the analysis of ICT adoption and diffusion pattern based upon a diffusion model (Rogers, 1995). The second is the analysis of the determinants using a

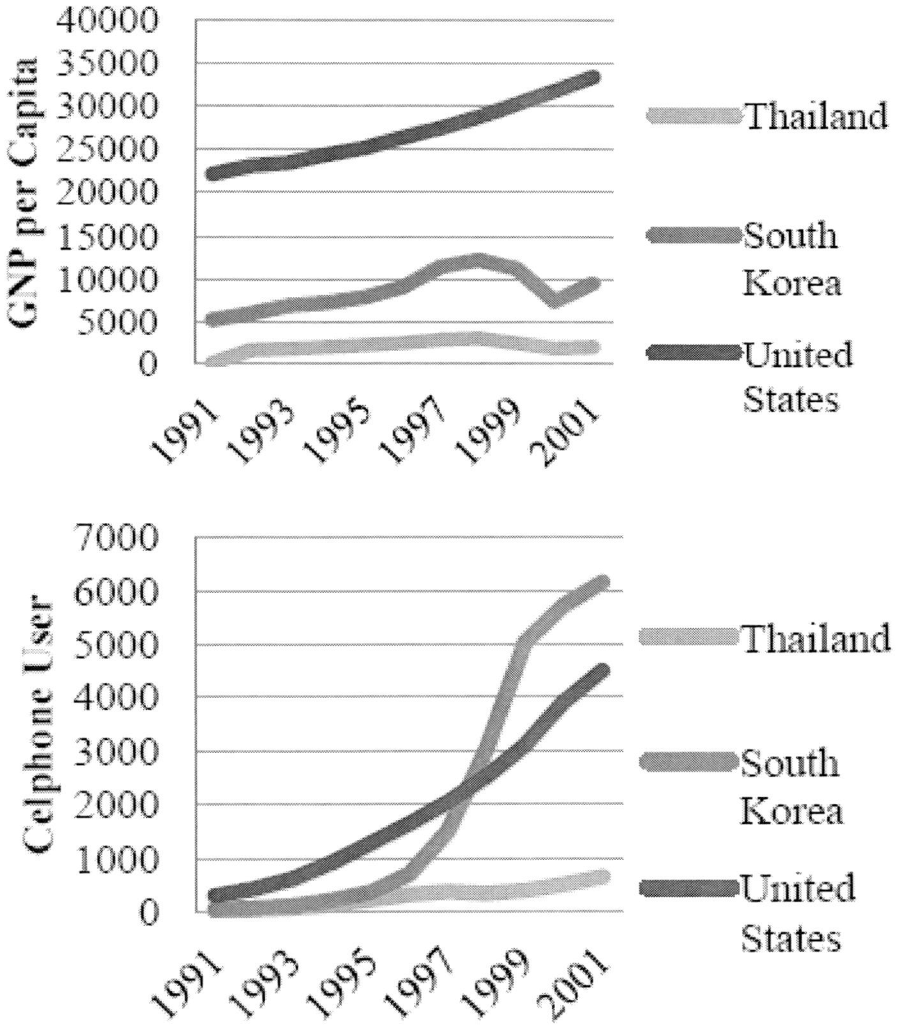

Figure 1. General Information of Thailand, South Korea and the United States.

unified model UTAUT (Venkatesh etal (2003) and the analysis of behaviors of champions (Russo and Kumer, 1992; Moore and Benbasat, 1991; Venkatesh et al., 2003).

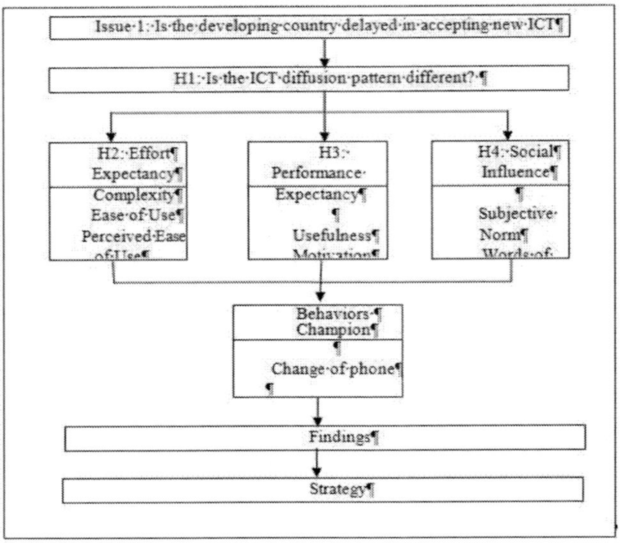

Figure 2. Research Model.

The third part is the "image" in the UTAIT model; however, we cannot measure the image factor using the same analysis method that was used for the second part. Therefore, we consider this analysis as the third phase instead of including it in the second component. The research model is summarized in Figure 2.

3.3. Research Hypotheses

3.3.1. ICT Diffusion Pattern

The main issue of the diffusion pattern is how ICT is adopted and assimilated by a person or an organization. This stream of research based on the DOI theory investigates the evaluation, adoption, and implementation process of innovation. Theories of the innovation process include those of Kwon and Zmud (1987), Rogers (1995), and others. Prescott and Conger (1995) called this kind of research the "stage research". While Rogers' model was the first innovation process model of organizational adoption and implementation, there have been many other stage models proposed over the years. Considerable work in this area has been undertaken by management scholars (Meyer and Goes, 1988) as well as ICT researchers, such as Kwon and Zmud (1987) and Cooper and Zmud (1990). They suggested a six-stage process model consisting of initiation, adoption, adaptation, acceptance, routinization, and infusion.

In this research, the model tested whether the ICT diffusion curves of developing, newly developed and developed countries have the same shapes. To compare the pattern of ICT adoption, the DOI model is used. The phases of the DOI model consist of introduction, growth, maturity and decline phase. But since the cellular phone is quite a new ICT product, we think that product is not yet in the decline phase. Therefore, the first three phases are considered in our model.

ICT acceptance may be defined differently. One definition treats the act of adopting the ICT as the initial decision to use it or not. Other research adopts a richer and more complex definition.

We define ICT acceptance as the time the individual purchased the cellular phone for the first time. To test the ICT diffusion pattern, we tested the following hypothesis:.

H1: The ICT adoption curve is the same according to the countries.

3.3.2. Diffusion Effects

We define the innovation diffusion effects as consisting of three sub-effects: effort expectancy, performance expectancy, and social influence.

3.3.2.1. Effort Expectancy

Complexity, ease of use, and perceived ease of use are used as factors of effort expectancy, which refers to the effect of technology innovation. Complexity is defined as the degree to which a system is perceived as relatively difficult to understand and use. We used a variety of functions of the cellular phone as an instrument.

Ease of use means the degree to which using an innovation is perceived as being difficult to use. We used the degree of ease of use to use for cellular phones as an instrument. Ease of use has been used by many previous researchers. For example, in Davis (1989), the ease of use is defined as "the degree to which a person believes that using a particular system would enhance her or his job performance".

Perceived ease of use is defined as the degree to which a person believes that using a system would be free of effort. We used the security, speed, and clearness of sound of the cellular phones as an instrument. Venkatesh (2000) presented and tested an anchoring and adjustment of technology based on a theoretical model of system-specific perceived ease of use as a determinant for technology adoption. His model proposed constructs related to control, intrinsic motivation, and emotion as general anchors for the formation of perceived ease of use regarding a new system. Also, Moore and Benbasat (1991) used relative advantage, ease of use, compatibility, image, result demonstrability, visibility and trialability.

Hypotheses on Effort Expectancy

To find out the effort expectancy, we hypothesized that the variety of functions, perceived quality, and perceived ease of use of the cellular telephone affects the adoption rate in each phase differently depending on the country.

H2-1: The variety of function of cellular phones in each phase of adoption is different for each type of country.

H2-2: Perceived quality of cellular phones in each phase of adoption is different from for each type of country.

H2-3: Perceived ease of use of cellular phones in each phase of adoption is different for each type of country.

3.3.2.2. Performance Expectancy

Performance expectancy refers to the diffusion effect caused by the increase of individual utility. Finding new applications for the new ICT is included in this category. According to Venkatesh et al. (2003), performance expectancy has five factors: perceived usefulness, extrinsic motivation, job-fit, relative advantage and outcome expectations. But, "relative advantage" does not fit when analyzing the cellular phone, because to measure the relative advantage, traditional phones and cellular phones should be compared, and we consider this comparison to be meaningless. Also, the factor "outcome expectation" is not considered, because job-fit can explain that effect in this research. Therefore, perceived usefulness, extrinsic motivation and job-fit are used to analyze the performance expectancy. Perceived usefulness means the degree to which a person believes that using a particular system would enhance his or her job performance. We used the possibility of increasing the quality of life as the expectation of a convenient life or the increase of income or achievements as an instrument. Extrinsic motivation is defined as the perception that users will want to perform an activity because it is perceived to be instrumental in achieving valued outcomes that are distinct from the activity itself, such as improved job performance, pay or promotions. We used the possibility of increases in income, payment or promotion as an instrument. Extrinsic motivation has a concept similar to self-efficacy, even though they are not exactly same.

Self-efficacy means "judgment of how well one can execute courses of action required to deal with prospective situations" (Bandura, 1986), and according to Bandura (1986), self-efficacy refers to individuals' beliefs about their ability and motivation to perform specific tasks. Compeau et al. (1999) showed that self-efficacy impacted an individual's affective and behavioral reactions to information technology. The concept of self-efficacy (Bandura, 1986) has been incorporated into IS research on technology adoption and use (Compeau and Higgins, 1995; Marakas et al., 1998; Staples et al., 1999).

Job-fit means refers to the capabilities of a system enhance an individual's job performance. We used the following items, such as reducing the job load and reduction in cost of living or work time, as instruments. To measure the performance expectancy, we hypothesized that extrinsic motivation of using the cellular telephone, its perceived usefulness, and the perceived job-fit of the cellular telephone affects the adoption rate in each phase differently depending on the country.

H3-1: The extrinsic motivation of using cellular phones in each phase of adoption is different for each type of country.

H3-2: Perceived usefulness on using cellular phones in each phase of adoption is different for each type of country.

H3-3: Perceived job-fit of cellular phones in each phase of adoption is different for each type of country.

3.3.2.3. Social Influences

Social influence means the effects caused by social environments, such as the upgrading of social status. Venkatesh et al. (2003) defined social influence as the degree to which an individual perceives it significant others believe he or she should use the new system. The effects of social influence processes were based on Theory of Planned Behavior (TPB). TPB is a well-established general theory of social psychology that asserts that specific salient beliefs influence given behavioral perceptions and subsequent actual behavior (Ajzen, 1985, 1991).

According to Venkatesh et al. (2003), social influences consist of three components: subjective norm, social factors and image. It exerts a significant direct effect on intent of use over and above the perceived usefulness and perceived ease of use for mandatory systems but not voluntarily systems. That is, people incorporate social influences into their own perception of usefulness and identification, in which people use a system to gain status and influence within their work group, and thereby improve their job performance.

Word of mouth (WOM) communications might be a highly important external variable as a powerful determinant of the adoption of technology. Consumers were affected more by WOM messages than by any other factor overall according to Webster (1991). Based on the prospect theory, several studies (Kahneman and Tversky, 1979; Einhornn and Hogarth, 1981; Aharony and Swary, 1980, Lang and Litzenberger, 1989; Michaely et al., 1995) detect stronger effects when information about a product is unfavorable rather than favorable, and when information is verbal rather than written (Herr et al., 1991). In addition, face-to-face WOM messages have proven to be powerful influences on consumer attitudes and behavior. Also, possible salient referents for the social normative component with respect to individual adoption of IT could be friends (Cale and Eriksen, 1994) and close peers of the potential adopter through their own personal interaction (Brancheau and Wetherbe, 1990).

Social factors are defined as the individual's internalization of the reference's subjective culture and specific interpersonal agreements that the individual has made with others in specific social situations. We used word of mouth, social factors, subjective norm and image to measure social influence. Since image was measured by a different method, it is discussed in the next section.

Social influence includes word of mouth, social factors, subjective norm and image. To find out social influences, we hypothesized that the effects of word of mouth, social factors, and subjective norm on using cellular telephone affects the adoption rate in each phase differently depending on the country.

H4-1: The word of mouth effect on using cellular phones in each phase of adoption is different for each type of country.

H4-2: The social factors on using cellular phones in each phase of adoption are different for each type of country.

H4-3: The subjective norm on using cellular phones in each phase of adoption is different for each type of country.

3.3.3. Image Effects

Studies repeatedly show that the most successful innovations were led by champions. Hoffer and Alexander (1992), Wynekoop, et al. (1992) and Russo and Kumar (1992) also emphasized the importance of the champion. Champions are leaders, or more specifically, they have the incessant drive and energy of leaders. Champion support for an innovation means that someone within the organization becomes a special advocate for the innovation, taking action to increase the probability of a successful adoption and implementation (Prescott and Conger, 1995).

In this research, we consider two types of champions: the early adopters and the frequent cellular phone or service company changers. The adopters of the introduction phase can be considered to be the opinion leaders or leading actors. However, the effects of the early adopters are considered in the performance expectancy. Therefore, in this paper, the frequent cellular phone or service company changers are considered as champion effects. Venkatesh et al. (2003) defined "image" as the degree to which use of an innovation is perceived to enhance one's image or status in one's social system. Therefore champions can be defined as people who are sensitive to their own good image.

There are different types of champions (Russo and Kumar, 1992; Prescott and Conger, 1995). In this research, we assume two types of champions: the early adopters and the cellular phones and the service company changers. To find out the effect of the champions, we hypothesized that the number of telephone changes in each phase of adoption is different depending on the type of country.

> H5: The number of telephone changes in each phase of adoption is different for each type of country.

4. Research Method

4.1 Data Collection

The unit of analysis in this study is individual. Data were collected in Thailand, South Korea, and the U.S. The survey instrument was first pilot tested by experts and modified questionnaires were mailed to 1,000 individuals.

In Thailand, 391 were returned with a 39.1% response rate. Seven responses were unusable because of accuracy issues. Out of 384, 336 responses showed ownership of cellular phones and 48 did not. In South Korea, 516 were returned (51.6% response rate). Three responses were unusable because of accuracy issues. Out of 513, 480 responses showed ownership of cellular phones and 33 did not. In the U.S., 188 were returned (18.8 % response rate). One response was excluded because of accuracy issues. Out of 187,165 responses showed ownership of cellular phones and 22 did not.

The adoption period is classified into the introduction, growth and maturity phase. The innovation diffusion cumulative curve has an S-shape curve. Therefore, in an introduction phase, the increase rate will continuously decrease. Also, at the beginning of the growth phase, the rate will increase and this increasing rate will continue until the end of the growth phase. At the beginning of the maturity phase, the adoption rate will abruptly decrease.

In the case of South Korea, the introduction phase occurred from 1989 to the fourth quarter of 1997 with 65 sample data for nine years. The growth phase occurred from the first quarter of 1998 to the second quarter of 2000, with 307 sample data for two and a quarter years. The maturity phase occurred from the third quarter of 2000 to the first quarter of 2003, with 108 sample data for three years.

In the case of the U.S., the introduction phase occurred from the second quarter of 1992 to the fourth quarter of 1997, with 33 sample data for nine years. The growth phase occurred from the first quarter of 1998 to the second quarter of 2000, with 79 sample data for two and a quarter years. And the maturity phase occurred from the third quarter of 2000 to the first quarter of 2003 with 53 sample data for two and three quarter years. For Thailand's data, the introduction phase occurred from 1987 to the fourth quarter of 1997, with 148 sample data for 11 years. The growth phase occurred from the first quarter of 1998 to the second quarter of 2000 with, 104 sample data for two and a quarter years. Also, the maturity occurred from the third quarter of 2000 to the first quarter of 2003, with 68 sample data for three years. One of the data analysis problems is that there is seasonality in the Thailand data. The number of adoptions of cellular phones in the first or second quarter of every year increased rapidly and returned to the normal trend. We doubt whether the cellular phone corporation had promotion programs during the first or second quarter of every year, but we were not able to obtain any information that they had promotion programs. We merely suspected that the symptom was due to some kind of custom of the country. The time series data are summarized in Figure 3.

4.2 Research Methods

4.2.1 Data Analysis

For reliability, Cronbach's alpha test was performed, and the results are summarized in Table 1.

For South Korea's data, all alpha coefficients were higher than the suggested value of 0.7 (Hair et al., 1998) except for the instrument "pressure of advertisement". For U.S. and Thailand's data, all alpha coefficients were higher than the suggested value of 0.7. Correlation matrices of the independent variables of each country are calculated and summarized in Tables 2, 3 and 4.

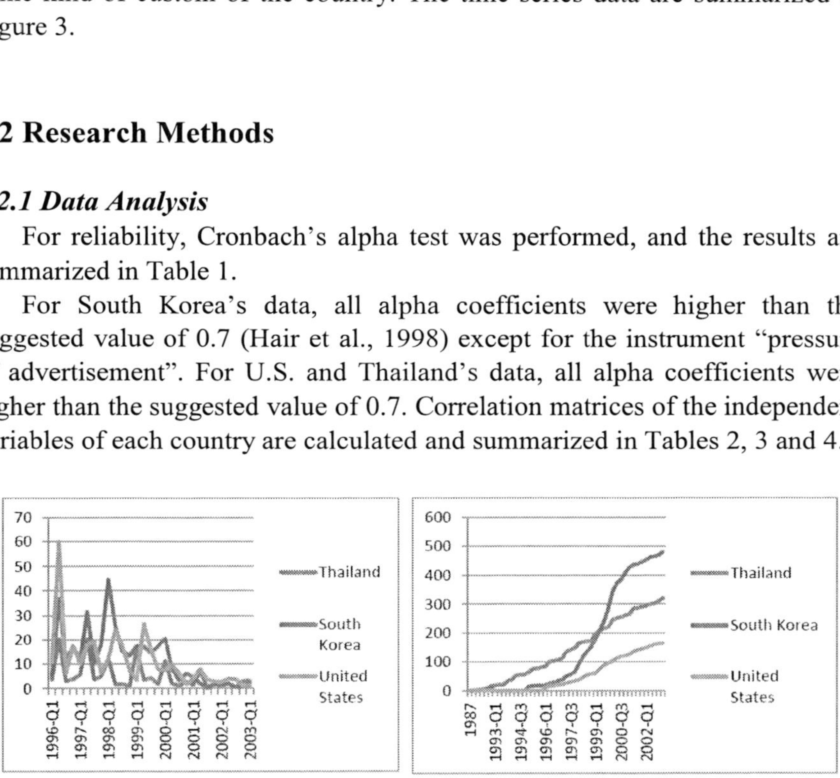

Figure 3. Time Series Data for the Three Countries.

Table 1. Results of Cronbach's Alpha Test

	Thailand	South Korea	U.S.
Increase Income	.874	.705	.900
Easy to Use	.873	.758	.900
Better Life	.785	.785	.785
Percentage of Neighbors	.873	.888	.902
Pressure from Neighbors	.875	.845	.900
Pressure from Advertisement	.872	.676	.905
Reduce Job Load	.872	.849	.897
Quality	.651	.651	.899
Variety of Functions	.871	.788	.899
Overall	.872	.76	.897

Table 2. Correlation Table (Thailand)

	1	2	3	4	5	6	7	8	9	10	11	12	13	14	15	16	17	18	19	20	21	22
PEU 1	1																					
PEU 2	.505**	1																				
PEU 3	.595**	.497**	1																			
COM 1	.146**	.215**	.135*	1																		
COM 2	.171**	.410**	.257**	.314**	1																	
EOU 1	.239**	.206**	.157**	.205**	.495**	1																
EOU 2	.154**	.147**	.081	.234**	.306**	.600**	1															
EMO 1	.236**	.147**	.185**	.049	.085	.077	.153**	1														
EMO 2	.373**	.214**	.271**	.145**	.086	.119*	.204**	.447**	1													
JTT 1	.549**	.463**	.557**	.183**	.281**	.133*	.163**	.198**	.251**	1												
JTT 2	.239**	.478**	.335**	.140*	.379**	.237**	.186**	.130*	.043	.447**	1											
JTT 3	.251**	.413**	.400**	.124*	.370**	.177**	.158**	.152**	.062	.461**	.721**	1										
PUS 1	.174**	.095	.160**	.085	.165**	.144*	.133*	.368**	.198**	.157**	.066	.085	1									
PUS 2	.153**	.170**	.104	.185**	.201**	.237**	.261**	.428**	.310**	.154**	.187**	.178**	.579**	1								
PUS 3	.244**	.145**	.170**	.175**	.080	.090	.162**	.360**	.297**	.157**	.094	.104	.473**	.611**	1							
WOM 1	.059	.152**	.081	.102	.209**	.154**	.155**	.166**	.169**	.113*	.118*	.093	.061	.189**	.091	1						
WOM 2	.095	.148**	.054	.068	.078	.116*	.070	.158**	.211**	.092	.069	.081	.057	.135*	.061	.784**	1					
SOF 1	.181**	.267**	.162**	.218**	.259**	.223**	.208**	.341**	.364**	.231**	.212**	.121**	.209**	.358**	.204**	.433**	.447**	1				
SOF 2	.039	.072	.054	.095	.022	-.034	.071	.010	.052	.012	-.109*	-.068	-.029	.034	-.001	.341**	.281**	.243**	1			
SUN 1	.330**	.259**	.225**	.189**	.171**	.181**	.139*	.276**	.304**	.275**	.151**	.172**	.136*	.249**	.268**	.423**	.370**	.402**	245**	1		
SUN 2	.257**	.185**	.195**	.296**	.242**	.143*	.090	.182**	.111*	.283**	.195**	.213**	.169**	.247**	.246**	.209**	.060	.057	.180**	.002	1	
SUN 3	.229**	.210**	.229**	.354**	.258**	.085	.057	.134*	.095	.307**	.189**	.214**	.154**	.216**	.227**	.198**	.084	.047	.144**	.038	.795**	1

** Correlation is significant at the 0.01 level (2-tailed)

* Correlation is significant at the 0.05 level (2-tailed)

Table 3. Correlation Table (South Korea)

	1	2	3	4	5	6	7	8	9	10	11	12	13	14	15	16	17	18	19	20	21	22
PEU 1	1																					
PEU 2	.56**	1																				
PEU 3	.467**	.561**	1																			
COM 1	.231**	.205**	.214**	1																		
COM 2	.075	.185**	.154**	.246**	1																	
EOU 1	.074	.101*	.099**	.143**	.372**	1																
EOU 2	.050	.110*	.155**	.203**	.350**	.597**	1															
EMO 1	.323**	.125**	.127**	.188**	.106*	.088	-.009	1														
EMO 2	.360**	.177**	.169**	.157**	.030	.076	.045	.343**	1													
JTT 1	.466**	.450**	.569**	.272**	.105*	.083	.099*	.282**	0.24	1												
JTT 2	.328**	.298**	.435**	.209**	.087	.066	.061	.191**	.143**	.581**	1											
JTT 3	.274**	.310**	.460**	.165**	.131**	.113**	.119*	.211**	.111*	.508**	.592**	1										
PUS 1	.277**	.162**	.140**	.251**	.129**	.056	.031	.428**	.211**	.278**	.208**	.199**	1									
PUS 2	.285**	.214**	.229**	.255**	.118*	.125**	.117*	.325**	.193**	.310**	.198**	.178**	.635**	1								
PUS 3	.396**	.294**	.248**	.319**	.120**	.143**	.101*	.412**	.271**	.334**	.251**	.191**	.637**	.704**	1							
WOM 1	.341**	.244**	.280**	.225**	.054	.080	.044	.333**	.214**	.342**	.229**	.322**	.238**	.303**	.357**	1						
WOM 2	.370**	.239**	.233**	.240**	.032	.115*	.054	.384**	.304**	.342**	.235**	.283**	.284**	.317**	.386**	.741**	1					
SOF 1	.289**	.255**	.240**	.179**	.171**	.077	.021	.263**	.190**	.275**	.199**	.227**	.256**	.334**	.338**	.325**	.378**	1				
SOF 2	.197**	.172**	.110**	.226**	.153**	.153**	.076	.130**	.199**	.172**	.127**	.170**	.161**	.246**	.263**	.201**	.232**	.306**	1			
SUN 1	.289**	.192**	.179**	.173**	.008	.090	.012	.359**	.227**	.229**	.217**	.288**	.259**	.238**	.263**	488**	.523**	.227**	.167**	1		
SUN 2	.022	.036	.069	.078	.075	-.051	-.048	.064	.085**	.042	0.034	.061	.082	.085	.100*	.061	.069	.089	.223**	.134**	1	
SUN 3	.011	.020	.092*	.071	.061	-.018	.007	.068	.061**	.067	0.023	.097*	.062	.048	.063	.051	.059	.056	.213**	.162**	.809**	1

** Correlation is significant at the 0.01 level (2-tailed)

* Correlation is significant at the 0.05 level (2-tailed)

Table 4. Correlation Table (U.S.)

	1	2	3	4	5	6	7	8	9	10	11	12	13	14	15	16	17	18	19	20	21	22
PEU 1	1																					
PEU 2	.601**	1																				
PEU 3	.831**	.634**	1																			
COM 1	.370**	.139	.313**	1																		
COM 2	.156	.207	.224*	.348**	1																	
EOU 1	.237*	.152	.175	.422**	.657**	1																
EOU 2	.267**	.219*	.218*	.301**	.602**	.744**	1															
EMO 1	.384**	.278**	.300**	.091**	-.045	.052	.078	1														
EMO 2	.593**	.352**	.487**	.165*	.027	.130	.183*	.679**	1													
JTT 1	.733**	.372**	.645**	.346**	.184	.224*	.197*	.419**	.650**	1												
JTT 2	.518**	.291**	.481**	.355**	.191	.238*	.330**	.314**	.454**	.595**	1											
JTT 3	.593**	.344**	.620**	.378**	.144	.277**	.348**	.275**	.469**	.605**	.733.**	1										
PUS 1	.449**	.182*	.354**	.276**	.095	.088	.150	.611**	.660**	.510.**	.413.**	.376.**	1									
PUS 2	.413**	.197*	.324**	.215**	.043	.003	.097	.627**	.665**	.475.**	.391.**	.335.**	.899.**	1								
PUS 3	.488**	.225**	.343**	.334**	.177	.139	.214*	.606**	.678**	.522.**	.429.**	.392.**	.856.**	.887.**	1							
WOM 1	.248**	.109	.182*	.095	-.052	.051	.138	.267**	.324**	.229.**	.218.**	.154.**	.318.**	.363.**	.393.**	1						
WOM 2	.404**	.243**	.349**	.124	-.012	.179	.256**	.354**	.461**	.386.**	.375.**	.353.**	.328.**	.371.**	.396.**	.739.**	1					
SOF 1	.305**	.203**	.263**	.079	.034	.069	.086	.440**	.508**	.364.**	.317.**	.277.**	.339.**	.377.**	.370.**	.400.**	.462.**	1				
SOF 2	.252**	.232**	.285**	-.046	-.028	-.002	.006	.378**	.445**	.310.**	.284.**	.249.**	.174*	.247.**	.220.**	.380.**	.471.**	.700.**	1			
SUN 1	.255**	.116	.171*	.070	-.065	.017	.139	.355**	.388**	.268.**	.275.**	.239.**	.389.**	.412.**	.453.**	706.**	.619.**	325.**	354.**	1		
SUN 2	.272**	.155	.203*	.469**	.213*	.190*	.155	.087	.193*	.252.**	.286.**	.289.**	.142	.107	.239.**	-.029	-.003	.049	.102	.03	1	
SUN 3	.317**	.178*	.211**	.459**	.224*	.175	.206*	.107	.250**	.291.**	.309.**	.311.**	.171*	.147	.304.**	.048	.088	.140	.124	.080	.912.**	1

**Correlation is significant at the 0.01 level (2-tailed).

*Correlation is significant at the 0.05 level (2-tailed).

Table 5. Survival Analysis with Descriptive Summary

Countries	Thailand						South Korea						United States					
Phase	Introduction		Growth		Maturity		Introduction		Growth		Maturity		Introduction		Growth		Maturity	
Variables	Wald.	Sig.	Wald.	Sig.	Wald.	Sig.	Wald.	Sig.	Wald.	Sig.	Wald.	Sig.	Wald.	Sig.	Wald.	Sig.	Wald.	Sig.
COM 1	0.39	0.03	0.55	0.46	3.69	0.06	3.71	0.05	2.68	0.1	2.64	0.08	0.9	0.04	1.9	0.02	3.86	0.35
COM 2	3.11	0.08	5.49	0.02	1.22	0.27	0.06	0.8	1.24	0.27	2.09	0.15	4.7	0.03	6.55	0.01	2.28	0.04
EOU 1	0.29	0.53	1.39	0.29	2	0.3	0.39	0.53	2.46	0.01	3.22	0.1	4.44	0.03	1.74	0	1.46	0.21
EOU 2	0.09	0.76	0.78	0.38	2.18	0.14	0.35	0.55	1.55	0.19	1.25	0.34	4.22	0.04	0.11	0.05	1.38	0.03
PEU 1	0.2	0.66	1.57	0.21	0.77	0.08	0.01	0.93	0.98	0	1.66	0.2	5.25	0.02	2.06	0.15	1.41	0.24
PEU 2	0.04	0.84	0.02	0.89	4.16	0.04	0.04	0.84	1.76	0.61	2.76	0.04	5.46	0.02	0.8	0.37	1.35	0.25
PEU 3	1.29	0.26	1.62	0.2	4.04	0.04	3.97	0.05	3.16	0.06	0.03	0.87	4.63	0.04	6.2	0.01	1.31	0.25
EMO 1	2.53	0.11	0.98	0.32	0.68	0.41	2.88	0.02	0.18	0.67	0.74	0.39	4.08	0.04	7.96	0.01	0.01	0.92
EMO 2	0.02	0.89	3.3	0.14	1.19	0.28	0.03	0.05	0.01	0.51	0.98	0.04	0.01	0.02	4.48	0.03	0.7	0.4
JFT 1	1.12	0.03	0.45	0.5	4.39	0.04	1.3	0.02	1.22	0.03	0.09	0.77	2.12	0.04	0.78	0.38	0.73	0.03
JFT 2	8.25	0	2.56	0.19	3.77	0.05	0.61	0.03	4.53	0.76	7.26	0.01	3.84	0.56	4.23	0.37	3.31	0.02
JFT 3	1.84	0.03	1.71	0.19	2.03	0	6.57	0.01	1.43	0.23	0.02	0.88	2.21	0.18	1.95	0.05	3.02	0.02
PUS 1	5.62	0.02	0.15	0.7	4.17	0.04	5.71	0.02	2.08	0.15	0.24	0.63	3.67	0.03	0.92	0.04	3.43	0.09
PUS 2	0.69	0.01	1.87	0.17	3.63	0.06	0.25	0.02	2.6	0.08	3.97	0.08	0.33	0	2.93	0.02	1.82	0.64
PUS 3	4.88	0.03	3	0.21	4.67	0.03	0.43	0.01	4.22	0.3	2.22	0.48	0.95	0.01	0.04	0.03	1	0.1
WOM 1	3.83	0.05	0.68	0.46	5.26	0.02	6.88	0.01	0.37	0.54	1.2	0.27	2.76	0.376.	0.01	0.92	0.33	0.09
WOM 2	3.96	0.05	1.07	0.3	4.16	0.04	0.26	0.01	2.99	0.02	5.11	0.11	0.89	0.16	0	0.96	0.33	0.57
SOF 1	0.09	0.77	1.56	0.21	3.51	0.03	3.75	0.05	0.98	0.32	0.22	0.64	3.11	0.05	1.31	0.02	2.18	0.14
SOF 2	0.18	0.67	0.77	0.34	2.65	0.02	1.93	0.02	1.03	0.11	1.3	0.26	2.9	0.57	3.7	0.05	4.62	0.22
SUN 1	4.46	0.04	2.1	0.15	4.88	0.03	1.72	0.01	3.33	0.1	1.68	0.09	0.01	0.91	0.13	0.72	0.09	0.76
SUN 2	1.86	0.04	1.98	0.16	3.24	0.1	1.93	0.02	2.5	0.01	3.81	0.05	2.39	0.2	3.89	0.27	3.32	0.06
SUN 3	2.39	0	0.7	0.4	4.25	0.04	6.57	0.01	0.04	0.85	3.1	0.08	4.02	0.05	4.12	0.04	3.68	0.06

4.2.2. Analysis Method

The survival analysis was used to compare the adoption rates of the countries. Originally, the survival analysis was concerned with the time from the initial treatment to death, hence the name, but it is applicable to many other areas than mortality. This method is often labeled differently in different fields, such as failure time analysis in engineering and event history analysis in sociology.

We used this method for the following two reasons. One is that the responses of non-adopters, as well as adopters, can be analyzed and the other is that the responses of each country, as well as comparisons of countries, can be obtained by this method.

For Thailand, the number of uncensored subjects was 48 and the number of the censored subjects 336. For South Korea, the number of the uncensored subjects was 33 and the number of the censored 480. For the U.S., the number of the uncensored subjects was 22 and the number of the censored 165. The uncensored data were classified into the introduction, growth and maturity phase.

To compare each phase, we assumed the data were censored at the end of the introduction phase, and the introduction group and non-introduction group were compared.

Then, we deleted the data of the introduction phase, assumed the data were censored at the end of the growth phase, and the data of the growth phase and non-growth phase were compared. Lastly, we deleted the data of the introduction and growth phases, and the data of the maturity phase and non-adopters were compared. The same procedures were repeated for each country (see Table 5).

To analyze the characteristics of champions, we surveyed the number of the telephone or service company changes. The frequency of cellular phone changes are summarized in Table 6. We found the rate of change was very high; therefore, we classified them as more frequent changers (people who changed phones more than twice) and less frequent changers (people who changed phones less than twice), instead of changers vs. non-changers. We defined the more frequent changers as the people who changed the phone or company more than once. We analyzed the data by using the LOGIT model.

Table 6. Results of Phone Change

Country		Thailand			South Korea			U.S.		
Phases / # of change		I	G	M	I	G	M	I	G	M
*	0	22	31	44	4	23	54	11	45	27
	1	2	14	9	8	73	46	0	13	12
*	2	9	11	10	14	87	17	6	15	10
*	3	13	14	8	16	53	10	3	5	3
	4	18	10	9	10	24	4	4	1	1
	5	7	8	2	11	14	2	6	0	0
	6	5	8	1	1	2	1	2	0	0
	7	1	4	0	0	2	0	0	0	0
	8	1	2	1	1	1	1	1	0	0
	9	1	1	0	0	0	0	0	0	0
	>10	1	1	0	0	0	1	0	0	0
# of **		56/80	59/104	31/84	53/65	183/279	36/136	22/33	21/79	14/53
% of **		70.0	56.7	36.9	81.5	65.6	26.5	66.7	26.6	26.4

(*: less frequent changers, **: more frequent changers).

Table 7. Comparison of ICT Diffusion Pattern

Countries	Wald. value	Significance	Results
Thailand vs. South Korea	202.56	0.00	Different
Thailand vs. U.S.	301.45	0.00	Different
South Korea vs. U.S.	4.153	0.04	Different

4.3 Hypotheses Testing

Hypothesis 1 is rejected. This means that the pattern of ICT adoption is different in each country at the significance level of 0.05 (Table 7). One interesting find is that the growth rate in the growth phase is very slow in Thailand. The portion of adopters is 46.3 % in Thailand, 13.5% in South Korea and 20.5 % in the U.S. at the beginning of the growth phase. However, the number of adopters increased by 472% in South Korea, and 239% in U.S., but only by 70% in Thailand in the growth phase. It can be interpreted that there was no explosive diffusion in Thailand.

The results of hypothesis 2 may be interpreted that the introductory adopters of Thailand and the U.S. consider the quality of ICT to be more important than the other effects, but the adopters at the introductory phase in South Korea did not. The adopters in South Korea care less about function. It can be guessed that such a property is the main source that makes South Korean such an ICT-developed country. The developing and developed countries show similar characteristics for ICT effects.

The results of hypothesis 3 may be interpreted that the adopters of the introductory phase considered the performance expectancy to be more important than other effects for adoption. However, as the adoption phase proceeded, the idea of the job-fit of adopters became weaker in newly developed and developed countries. It is hard to interpret the results of a developing country, because the behaviors of the adopters in the growth phase appear to be completely different than that of the adopters in the introductory and maturity phases.

The results of hypothesis 4 may be interpreted that the adopters of the introductory phase think social influence is more important than any other criteria for adoption.

However, as the adoption phase proceeded, the idea of social influences affecting adopters became weaker in the newly developed and developed countries. In the developing country, the behavior of the adopters in the growth phase seems inconsistent and irrational. The results of hypotheses 2, 3, and 4 are summarized in Table 8.

Hypothesis 5-1 is accepted. The number of telephone changes is different between Thailand and South Korea, Thailand and the U.S. but not between South Korea and the U.S. Hypothesis 5-2 is accepted. The number of telephone changes is different between Thailand and South Korea, Thailand and the U.S. but not between South Korea and the U.S. Hypothesis 5-3 is rejected in all of the three countries. This means we cannot say if the number of telephone changes is different. Hypothesis 5 means the pattern of change of cellular phones is different in the countries at the introductory and growth phases, but is the same at the maturity phase. How much different is explained in tables 9 and 10.

Table 8. Results of Hypothesis 2, 3, and 4

			Thailand			South Korea			U.S.		
Sub-Category	Factors	Instruments	Intro.	Growth	Maturity	Intro.	Growth	Maturity	Intro.	Growth	Maturity
Effort Expectancy	Complexity	Variety of Functions	Yes						Yes	Yes	
	Perceived quality	Quality (Security, Speed Clearness of Sound)							Yes	Yes	
	Perceived Ease of Use	Ease of Use			Yes				Yes		
Performance Expectancy	Extrinsic Motivation (Self-efficacy)	Better Life				Yes			Yes	Yes	
	Perceived Usefulness	Increase Income	Yes		Yes	Yes					Yes
	Job-Fit	Reduce Job Load	Yes		Yes	Yes			Yes	Yes	
Social Influence	Word of Mouth	Pressure from Neighbors	Yes		Yes	Yes					
	Social Factors	Pressure from Advertisement			Yes	Yes				Yes	
	Subjective Norm	Percentage of Neighbors	Yes		Yes	Yes					

Table 9. Comparison of Phone Change by Country

Countries	Phase	Significance	Results
Thailand	Introduction - Growth	0.00	Different
	Introduction - Maturity	0.00	Different
	Growth - Maturity	0.012	Different
South Korea	Introduction - Growth	0.00	Different
	Introduction - Maturity	0.00	Different
	Growth - Maturity	0.00	Different
U.S.	Introduction - Growth	0.00	Different
	Introduction - Maturity	0.00	Different
	Growth - Maturity	0.00	Different

Table 10. Comparison of Phone Change by Phase

Countries	Phase	Significance	Results
Introduction	Thailand vs. South Korea	0.00	Different
	Thailand vs. U.S.	0.028	Different
	South Korea vs. U.S.	0.87	Not different
Growth	Thailand vs. South Korea	0.00	Different
	Thailand vs. U.S.	0.00	Different
	South Korea vs. U.S.	0.727	Not different
Maturity	Thailand vs. South Korea	0.378	Not different
	Thailand vs. U.S.	0.055	Not different
	South Korea vs. U.S.	0.279	Not different

We found the characteristics of champions are different. Frequent changers are concerned about social influences in South Korea and Thailand, but not in the U.S. The summary is in Table 11.

CONCLUSION

The results of this study shed interesting light on ICT adoption. We found that the patterns of ICT adoptions are different according to country. Thailand has a long introduction phase compared to that of the other two countries. The growth phase of Thailand also ended earlier compared to the other two countries. As a consequence, the increase rate of ICT adoption is low. It can be interpreted that the explosive growth of the adoption environment was not

Table 11. LOGIT model of Champions

		Thailand	South Korea	U.S.
Characteristic of Champion	Effort Expectancy	N/A	N/A	Ease of Use (sig. = .032)
	Performance Expectance	Motivation (sig. = .038)	N/A	Motivation (sig. = .039), Perceived Usefulness ** (sig. = .034), Job-fit** (sig. = .025)
	Social Influence	Social Factors** (sig. = .017)	Social Factors** (sig. = .013), Subjective Norm** (sig. = .032)	N/A
	Persona	Age** (sig. = .026)	Age** (sig. = .015)	N/A

(*: p<.1, **: p<.05, ***: p<.01).

created even though the rate of the introduction phase is similar to that of the other countries. That can be the critical factor that prevents the development of the ICT industry in developing countries.

We found factors that differentiate the ICT adoption pattern. First, the adopters of South Korea seem to be in a rush to adopt new ICT and that may be a positive influence in the development of the ICT industry. The critical factors of South Korean adopters are performance expectancy and social influences. For them, effort expectancy seems to be less important. Furthermore, performance expectancy and social influences disappeared for adopters in the growth and maturity phases. It can be interpreted that for South Korean adopters, the expectation of quality is not as high. It seems that they do not consider the quality of technology seriously.

The second finding is that the pattern of the growth phase and behaviors of the adopters of the growth phase in developing countries are quite different from those of the other two countries. We found some diffusion effects in the introduction and maturity phases but could not find any type of diffusion effect in the growth phase. We assume that this fact is the main cause delaying the development of the ICT industry in developing countries. It means the adoption of the introduction phase cannot drive the explosive adoption of the growth phase. Therefore, the potential adopters of the growth phase cannot find any purchasing motivation. Effort expectancy, performance expectancy, and social influence effects appear in the maturity phase. We think the adopters of the maturity phase are logical and consider every factor.

The third finding is that the initial adoption time of the three countries is similar. Some adopters in Thailand adopted the cellular phone earlier than the adopters of the other two countries. It means "there is no time gap" in the introduction of new ICT among countries. We can infer the following fact from this phenomenon: the digital divide can be caused not only by diffusion of ICT among countries but by internal environments. This is meaningful, as finding the cause is useful in reducing the digital divide gap.

The fourth finding is that the adopters of the developed country are very reasonable and consistent. They consider all types of diffusion effects in the introduction and the growth phases. One remarkable phenomenon is that they do not consider technology factors in the maturity phase. We guess the reason is that they assume the technology is trustworthy, because many people already use ICT products.

The last finding is that we cannot find any common reason for changing phones. The reasons for changing phones appear to be different depending on the country. However, social influences were found to be more important than effort and performance expectancy in Thailand and South Korea. We considered the fact that image may be the main factor in the frequency of change. Young adopters are likely to change their phone more easily in Thailand and South Korea. Also, we found age to be a factor in changing cellular phones. We infer that this phenomenon is a cultural factor. Usually parents pay for the cost of changing and maintaining phones in Thailand and South Korea. The main reason for U.S. phone users switching phones is performance expectancy. This result again shows that users of developed countries are pragmatic. Based upon the above analysis, we suggest the push strategy to motivate the potential growth adopters, because the adoption rate in the growth phase is low.

The limitations of this research are as follows: first, South Korea and Thailand suffered the Asian financial crisis, and the adoption pattern seems to have been affected by this crisis. Second, the data for Thailand is affected by seasonality. Many adopters bought a cellular phone in the first or second quarter of every year. Our estimate is that they may receive a monetary bonus at work or that some telephone companies may have active promotional programs at the end or beginning of the year. To reduce seasonality, we averaged the value of data to normalize the seasonality; however, we cannot say we removed this effect.

Third, only one country represents each category. For future research, analysis of other developing countries is needed. However, we believe the results of this research can be used to bridge the digital divide between developing and developed countries. Also, the lessons of newly developed countries can be used in building strategies for ICT adoption on a macro level and reduce the digital divide gap between developing countries and developed countries.

REFERENCES

Agarwal, R. , (2000). Individual acceptance of information technologies.In R.B. Zmud (Ed.), *Framing the domains of IT Management: Projecting the future through the past,* (pp. 85-104). Cincinnati, OH: Pinnaflex Educational Resources.

Aharony, J., and Swary, I. (1980). Quarterly dividend and earnings announcements and stockholders' return: An empirical analysis, *Journal of Finance*, 35(1), 1-12.

Ajzen, I. From Intentions to Actions: A Theory of Planned Behavior, in *Action Control: From Cognition to Behavior*, J. Kuhl and J Beckmann, eds.), Heidelberg, *Springer,* (1985) 11-39.

Ajzen, I. (1991). The Theory of Planned Behavior, *Organizational Behavior and Human Decision Processes,* 50, 179-211.

Bandura, A. (1986). *Social Foundations of Thought and Action*, Englewood Cliffs, NJ: Prentice Hall.

Brancheau, J. C., and Wetherbe, J. C. (1990). The adoption of spreadsheet software:Testing innovation diffusion theory in the context of end-user computing, *Information Systems Research*, 1(2), 115-143.

Burkhardt, M.E., andBrass, D. J. (1990). Changing patterns or patterns of change:The effects of a change in technology on social network structure and power,*Administrative Science Quart*erly, 35, 104-127.

Cale, E. J. Jr., and Eriksen, S. E. (1994). Factors affecting the implementation outcome of a mainframe software package: A longitudinal approach, *Information and Management*, 26, 165-175.

Compeau, D.R., andHiggins, C. A. (1995). Application of social cognitive theory to training for computer skills, *Information Systems Research*, 6(2), 118-143.

Compeau, D. R., Higgins, C. A., and Huff, S. (1999). Social cognitive theory and individual reactions to computing technology: A longitudinal study, *MIS Quarterly*, 23(2), 145-158.

Cooper, R. B., and Zmud, R. W. (1990). Information technology implementation research: a technology implementation research: A technological diffusion approach, *Management Science*, 36(2), 123-139.

Davis, F. D. (1989). Perceived usefulness, perceived ease of use, and user acceptance of information technology, *MIS Quarterly*, 13(3), 319-340.

Einhorn, H. J., and Hogarth R. M. (1981). Behavioral decision theory: Processes of judgment and choice, *Annual Review of Psychology*, 32, 53-88.

Fichman, R.G. The Diffusion and Assimilation of Information Technology Innovations, *Framing the Domains of IT Management: Projecting the Future through the Past.* R.B. Zmud, ed. Pinnaflex Educational Resources, Inc., Cincinnati, OH., 2000.

Gallivan, M. (2001). Organizational adoption and assimilation of complex technological innovations: Development and application of a new framework,*DataBase*, 32(3), 51-85.

Hair J.F.Jr., Anderson, R. E., Tatham, R. L., and Black, W. C. (1998). *Multivariate data analysis*, Upper Saddle River, NJ: Pearson Education.

Grover, V., Fiedler, K., and Teng, J. (1997). Empirical evidence on Swanson's tri-core model of information systems innovation, *Information Systems Research,* 8(3), 273-287.

Herr, P. M., Kardes, F. R., and Kim, J. (1991). Effects of word of mouth and product-attribute information on persuasion: An accessibility-diagnosticity perspective, *Journal of Consumer Research,* 17, 454-462.

Hoffer, J. A., and Alexander, M .B. (1992). The diffusion of database machines. *DataBase*, 23(2), 13-19.

Kahneman, D., and Tversky, A. (1979). Prospect theory: An analysis of decisions under risk, *Econometrica*, 47, 508-522.

Kwon, T.H., and Zmud, R. W. (1987). Unifying the fragmented models of information systems implementation. In J. R. Boland, R. Hirschheim, (Eds.) *Critical Issues in Information Systems Research* (pp. 227-251). New York, NY: John Wiley and Sons Ltd.

Lang, L., and Litzenberger, R. H. (1989). "Dividend announcements: Cash flow signaling vs. free cash flow hypothesis?" *Journal of Financial Economics*, 24, 181-191.

Marakas, G. M., Yi, M. Y., and Johnson, R. D. (1998). The multilevel and multifaceted character of computer self-efficacy: Toward clarification of the construct and an integrative framework for research, *Information Systems Research*, 9(2), 126-163.

Meyer, A.D., and Goes, J. B. (1988). Goes organizational assimilation of innovations: A multilevel contextual analysis,*Academy of Management Journal*, 31(4), 897-923.

Moore, G.C., andBenbasat, I. (1991). Development of an instrument to measure the perceptions of adopting an information technology innovation,*Information Systems Research*, 2(3), 192-222.

Prescott, M.B., andConger, S. A. (1995). Information technology innovations: A classification by IT locus of impact and research approach,*Database,* 26(2-3), 20-41.

Rogers, E. M. (1995). *Diffusion of Innovations*, New York: Free Press.

Russo, N.L., and Kumar, K. (1992). Studying the impact of information technology innovations in organizations: The influence of individual characteristics, innovation characteristics, and the innovation introduction process. In K. E. Kendall, K. Lyytinen, J. I. Degross (Eds.)*The impact of computer-supported technologies on information systems development.* Minneapolis, MN: Elsevier Science Publications.

Ryan, B., and Gross, N. C. (1943). The Diffusion of hybrid seed corn in two Iowa communities, *Rural Sociology,* 8(1) 15-24.

Staples, D. S., Hulland, J. S., and Higgins, C. A. (1999). A self-efficacy theory explanation for the management of remote workers in virtual organizations, *Organization Science*, 10(6), 758-776.

Swanson, E.B. (1994). Information systems innovations among organizations,*Management Science*, 40(9), 1069-1092.

Taylor, S., and Todd, P. (1995). Understanding information technology usage: A test of computing models, *Information Systems Research*, 6(2) 144-176.

Venkatesh, V. (2000). Determinants of perceived ease of use: Integrating control, intrinsic motivation, and emotion into the technology acceptance model,*Information Systems Research*, 11(4), 342-365.

Venkatesh, V., Morris, M. G., Davis, G. B., and Davis, F. (2003). User acceptance of information technology: Toward a unified view, *MIS Quarterly*, 27(3)l 425-478.

Webster, C. (1991). Influences upon consumer expectations of services, *Journal of Services Marketing*, 5(1), 5-17.

Wynekoop, J. L., Senn, J. A., and Conger, S. A. (1992). The implementation of CASE tools: An innovation diffusion approach. In K. E. Kendall, K. Lyytinen, J. I. Degross (Eds.), *The impact of computer-supported technologies on information systems development* (pp. 25-41). Minneapolis, MN: Elsevier Science Publications.

In: South Korea ISBN: 978-1-61942-377-0
Editors: A. L. Hines and D. O. Mullins

Chapter 2

SOUTH KOREA'S DEMOGRAPHIC DILEMMA

Ben Brown[1]
Department of Criminal Justice,
University of Texas at Brownsville, Texas, US

The demographic composition of any nation's populace is in constant flux, with new challenges arising along with demographic shifts. Few nations, however, face as serious a quandary as does South Korea at the dawn of the 21st century. The South Korean populace is rapidly becoming disproportionately elderly, with far too few births occurring each year to maintain a solidly youthful population base. To provide an illustrative description of the problematic shift, consider some basic geometric shapes.

First, imagine a robust population as a pyramid-shaped beaker with a broad base that decreases in circumference as the beaker ascends in height. At the base, the broadest area of the beaker, are the youngest members of the populace, with the working age demographic immediately above them and—owing to the forces of nature (e.g., disease and congenital health issues) and the ordinary dangers that accompany modern life (e.g., automobile accidents, fires, homicides, and workplace fatalities)—the size of the working age

[1] Email: ben.brown@utb.edu.

demographic slowly contracts as does our hypothetical pyramid-shaped population beaker as it ascends. At the top, the point at which the perimeter of the beaker is most constricted, are the elderly.

Now imagine a population with maturational features similar to a simple jar, a cylindrical shaped container with slight constrictions at the top and bottom. At the base of the jar, an area with a circumference slightly smaller than the mid-section, are the youngest members of the population, with the working age demographic constituting the large mid-section of the jar immediately above them. At the very top, where the circumference is equal to that at the base, is the elderly population. If the South Korean populace is conceptualized in terms of basic geometric shapes, rather than resembling a pyramid-shaped beaker, it is beginning to resemble a jar. Over time, if there is no reversal in the current demographic trends, the jar will slowly transform into a funnel, with a sizeable elderly demographic weighing down on a shrinking population of working age persons and children.

The low fertility rate and rapid aging of the population are relatively recent developments in South Korea. In the mid-1900s, following the hardships of Japanese colonization (1910-1945) and the devastation of the Korean War (1950-1953), South Korea was an industrially unsophisticated rural society with a predominantly agricultural economy (Cummings, 1997). As is typically the case with poorly developed nations, in the 1950s and early 1960s South Korea had a high fertility rate. Though record-keeping practices at the time were relatively crude, it is estimated that the fertility rate in South Korea was in excess of six children per woman (Haub, 2010). In short, around the middle of the 20th century the South Korean populace resembled, utilizing the aforementioned geometric concepts, a pyramid-shaped beaker.

Recognizing the potential problems associated with overpopulation, in the 1960s the South Korean government began family planning operations. By means of public information campaigns, the populace was encouraged to have fewer children. As the nation swiftly industrialized there was a decrease in the fertility rate, as normally accompanies the social processes of industrialization. With a shift from an agrarian economy to an industrial economy, children no longer serve as immediate assets to a family. Whereas in an agrarian society children are viewed as people who will help work the land, in an industrial society wherein adults labor in factories and offices, kids are seen as people of no immediate productive value who must be fed and cared for (Cruickshank, 1981; Sharar, 1990).

By the 1970s, when South Korea had matured into an industrial society, the fertility rate had dropped to roughly four and a half children per woman and by the 1980s the fertility rate had dropped below the basic population replacement rate of two children per woman (Cummings, 1997; Haub, 2010; OECD Directorate of Employment, Labour, and Social Affairs, 2011; Sleebos, 2003). Since that time the fertility rate has continued to decrease, presently hovering somewhere around 1.2 or 1.3 children per woman, while the proportion of the population constituted of elderly adults has increased, with roughly a tenth of the population being 65 years of age or older (H. S. Lee, 2006; Y. J. Yoon, 2006a, 2006b). As of this writing South Korea has one of the lowest fertility rates in the world. Although there remains some academic debate as to which nation has the absolute lowest fertility rate and while the vast majority of the world's most advanced nations such as Australia, Canada, Denmark, Germany, Japan, the United Kingdom, and the United States have fertility rates below the basic replacement rate of two children per woman, some of the most recent demographic estimates available suggest that South Korea has the lowest fertility rate on the planet (OECD Directorate of Employment, Labour, and Social Affairs, 2011). The fertility rate has been so low for so long that there are not enough children to justify the expense of operating some of the nation's schools. Education officials in a number of rural areas have had to close schools and, in 2011, education officials in Seoul began examining schools throughout the city to ascertain which schools could be merged together, with students from schools with the lowest enrollments being moved to other schools in order that the schools with the fewest students could be closed (Na, 2011).

A decrease in the fertility rate normally accompanies industrialization and modernization (Calhoun, 1945; Cruickshank, 1981), but the reduction in the fertility rate in South Korea has been, by any standard, phenomenal and may have dire consequences if not corrected (Seo, 2006). As to the query of why the fertility rate in South Korea has plunged to perilously low levels, there are a number of factors to take into consideration. First, with the basic processes of modernization, there is inevitably a decrease in the fertility rate. As heretofore discussed, as societies evolve beyond a basic agrarian form, children come to require more and more care. Additionally, the time required for a full transition from childhood, through adolescence, into young adulthood increases. Thus, adults tend to have fewer children in order that the requisite care may be afforded to the young.

Additionally, as societies modernize there is typically an increase in the basic rights enjoyed by women. In contrast to the historical global norm of women being denied access to education, paid employment, and the opportunity to serve in leadership roles in public and private enterprises, with modernization comes strides toward gender equality. As women are afforded the opportunity to engage in meaningful participation in a variety of career fields, they tend to postpone marriage and motherhood and, ultimately, have fewer children. These tendencies have been further facilitated by advances in birth control, legal access to medically safe abortion procedures, and the ability of women to determine when or when not to use birth control and/or abort a fetus. In short, as the protection of women's basic rights increases and as women gain control over their own sexuality and reproductive capacities, there is typically a reduction in fertility rates. These social phenomena have had the same negative impact on fertility rates in South Korea as in other developed nations.

Next, there is the population density. Although fertility rates in South Korea have been below the basic population reproduction level of two children per woman for well over a decade, it remains one of the most densely populated nations on the planet. With a total area of less than 100,000 square kilometers (about the size of the state of Indiana in the United States), the nation has a total population of roughly fifty million people. Further intensifying the density is the fact that the South Korean citizenry is exceptionally urbane, with almost half of the nation's population residing in the greater Seoul-Gyeonggi Province metropolitan area (J. H. Kim, 2007). In such an environment, housing is compact and costly. The sheer physical confines of the typical home in South Korea, especially when considered in light of the increase in the basic standard of living that accompany modernization, have no doubt served to deter couples from having many children.

Finally, there is the deep respect for education embedded in the Korean culture and the high costs associated with education in South Korea. The importance that South Koreans place on education has exacerbated the costs of childrearing in terms of time, energy, and money. A careful tour of any sizeable city in South Korea will reveal a variety of educational institutes which typically specialize in a particular subject such as English as a Second Language, mathematics, science, or music and cater to juveniles. The small buses which serve to taxi kids to and from these institutes are a ubiquitous presence in the late afternoon and early evening in many urban areas. As children mature into teenagers, an increasing portion of each day is dedicated to academics. It is not at all unusual to see high school students slugging home from their studies at nine or ten o'clock in the evening (and, in some cases, even later than that). The costs associated with education in South Korea, especially the tuition at the private institutes which many youths attend, can place a financial strain on couples and serve as a deterrent to having additional children.

In brief, the decline in the birth rate and aging of the South Korean populace is the result of: (i) the basic social processes of modernization and reduction of the economic productivity of juveniles, (ii) an increase in the social status and power of women and advances in birth control technology, (iii) the urban character of the populace and concomitant population density, and (iv) the high value placed on education and the costs associated with a quality education. From a public policy standpoint, these are tough obstacles to overcome. For example, it would be absurd to suggest that women should no longer be allowed to pursue advanced university degrees and be prohibited from serving in administrative or managerial positions in order to encourage them to have more children. Similarly, it would be ludicrous to argue that parents should be less concerned about the education and future welfare of their children in an effort to cut down on the costs associated with child rearing and thereby encourage people to have more kids.

Although the South Korean government has implemented policies designed to encourage people to have more children (e.g., tax breaks for having more than two kids), the nation's fertility rate has remained among the lowest in the world (Park, 2006; Seo, 2006). As a result, South Korean officials have been considering alterations of the nation's immigration policies in an effort to address the rapid aging and impending reduction of the population (T. H. Kim, 2011; Jung, 2006). The liberalization of South Korea's immigration policies is arguably the only viable option for addressing the nation's current demographic quandary, as all other efforts to address the dismal fertility rate have thus far failed to have any significant impact. However, any new policies or programs which encourage foreigners to permanently immigrate to South Korea will also generate some social turmoil, especially in terms of fostering racial/ethnic bigotry and discrimination.

The Koreans have long been a very homogenous group and are not known for welcoming outsiders into their ranks. In South Korea there is considerable discrimination against persons from other nations and even against North Korean defectors. Despite the fact that North Koreans and South Koreans have a shared cultural, linguistic, and ethnic heritage, within South Korea there remains a bias against North Koreans and, as a result, many North Koreans (who typically went through considerable hardships to escape from North Korea into South Korea) have great difficulties adjusting to life in South Korea (I. J. Yoon, 2011). Prejudice against immigrants from other nations and against children born to mixed couples is arguably even greater than the prejudice against North Koreans as foreigners from outside of the Korean peninsula have discernibly different racial/ethnic characteristics, often have palpable difficulties with the Korean language, and are unfamiliar with cultural norms (Carpenter, 2006; J. W. Lee, 2006).

In point of fact, growing problems associated with prejudice against foreigners have already begun developing in South Korea, especially in the rural parts of the nation. Owing to some of the heretofore discussed issues—in particular, the modernization of the nation, the empowerment of women, and the urbane character of the South Korean populace—many farmers in South Korea have found it difficult to marry. As females gained access to education and career opportunities, an increasing number of women from rural areas flocked to the cities, the end result being that farmers (who are necessarily tied to rural farm lands) have had trouble finding brides. Many farmers thus took it upon themselves to liberalize the nation's immigration policies by means of the somewhat controversial practice of finding suitable spouses from international match-making services: A practice most commonly known as the "mail order bride." During the first decade of the 21st century, more than a tenth of all marriages in South Korea involved an immigrant, typically the bride, with sizeable numbers of young women coming from less developed Asian nations such as China, Vietnam, and the Philippines to marry South Korean men (T. J. Kim, 2011; Y. J. Kim, 2011; H. S. Lee, 2006b, 2011; Y. J. Yoon, 2006c).

Many of these women face great hardships as they try to adjust to life in South Korea. In addition to the unavoidable psychological agonies associated with separation from family and friends, a fundamental change in diet, the acquisition of a new language, and limited (if any) access to the entertainment of their native culture (games, music, movies, etc.), these women are often discriminated against by the local South Korean citizenry in the areas in which they live and their bi-ethnic children often face harassment from their classmates in the schools (Jung, 2006; R. Kim, 2011; T. J. Kim, 2011; Y.J. Kim, 2011). In the event that South Korea opens its doors to more foreigners, allowing them to not only reside in the nation with a work visa, but also to become permanent residents or nationalized citizens, there will likely be some public backlash and an increase in discriminatory behaviors against the foreigners and their offspring.

In summary, the low fertility rate among and aging of the South Korean population are issues of fundamental importance. If the current population trends are not altered, the South Korean people will face enormous economic hardships in the coming decades. Because a reversal of the causes of the low fertility rate (e.g., modernization, advances toward gender equality) is not viable, the single best option for addressing South Korea's population woes appears to be a liberalization of the nation's immigration policies. Such a measure, however, will likely generate new problems in terms of racial/ethnic discrimination. Because the South Korean populace has historically been very homogenous, widespread racial/ethnic prejudice and discrimination are problems the citizenry has little experience contending with. In order to facilitate a smooth transition from a homogenous population to a diverse and multicultural populace, now is the time for South Korean scholars and officials to begin developing policies and programs (e.g., public information campaigns, laws banning discriminatory practices, educational curriculum) to reduce discriminatory behaviors before such behaviors become deeply embedded in the norms of the populace. While such a task will not be easy, in the long run a proactive process of policy and program development which anticipates the problems associated with bigotry and prejudice will undoubtedly prove superior to a reactive process of waiting until discriminatory practices result in dire consequences and then attempting to address the issue.

REFERENCES

Calhoun, A. W. (1945). A social history of the American family. New York, NY: Barnes and Noble.

Carpenter, C. (2006, October 26). Fitting in: Raising foreign or mixed-race children in Korea. *Korea Times*, p. 11.

Cruickshank, M. (1981). Children and industry: Child health and welfare in North-west textile towns during the nineteenth century. Manchester: Manchester University Press.

Cummings, B. (1997). *Korea's place in the sun*. New York: W. W. Norton and Company.

Haub, C. (2010). Did South Korea's population policy work too well? Washington, DC: Population Reference Bureau. Available online at: http://www.prd.org/Articles/2010/koreafertility.aspx?p=1.

Jung, S. K. (2006, April 6). Bills to protect mixed race Koreans. *Korea Times*, p. 2.

Kim, J. H. (2007, November 19). Population jumps past 50 million mark. Korea Herald. Retrived online from LexisNexis database.

Kim, T. H. (2011, July 11). Korea mulls new office for migrant policy. *Korea Times*, p. 1.

Kim, T. J. (2011, July 26). Taking on challenges key to smooth settlements here. *Korea Times*, p. 5.

Kim, R. (2011, July 15). Most immigrant women seek Korean names. *Korea Times*, p. 3.

Kim, Y. J. (2011, July 13). Dreams, despair of 'migrant brides' in Paju. *Korea Times*, p. 5.

Lee, H. S. (2011, August 1). Int'l marriages account for 10.5% of newlyweds in 2010. *Korea Times*, p. 3.

Lee, H. S. (2006a, December 14). Population growth at world bottom. *Korea Times*, p. 11.

Lee, H. S. (2006b, October 25). 14,000 foreign women reside in rural area. *Korea Times*, p. 2.

Lee, J. W. (2006, October 30). North Korean defectors to reach 10,000 next year. *Korea Times*, p. 13.

Na, J. J. (2011, July 15). Schools mull merger amid dwindling students. *Korea Times*, p. 3.

OECD Directorate of Employment, Labor, and Social Affairs. (2011). Fertility Rates. Paris, France: Organisation for Economic Cooperation and Development Family Database. Available at: *http://www.oecd.org /dataoecd/37/59/40192107.pdf.*

Park, Y. B. (2006, May 18). How to promote childbirth. *Korea Times*, p. 8.

Rahn, K. (2006, August 31). 60% of foreign spouses are Chinese. *Korea Times*, p. 3.

Seo, D. S. (2006, June 21). Korea adopts social pact to battle low birthrate. *Korea Times*, p. 4.

Sharar, S. (1990). Childhood in the middle ages. London: Routledge.

Sleebos, J. E. (2003). Low fertility rates in OECD countries: Facts and policy responses (OECD Social, Employment, and Migration Working Paper 15). Paris, France: Publications Service of the Organisation for Economic Cooperation and Development. Available online at: *http://www.oecd .org/dataoecd/13/38/16587241.pdf.*

Yoon, I. J. (2011, July 29). Ethnic and multicultural dimensions of South Koreans' perceptions of North Korean migrants. Presentation given at the

2011 Joint Faculty Seminar of Korea University and International Summer Campus. Seminar hosted and sponsored by Korea University BK21 Project Group for Conflict Society, Korea University Institute of Social Research, and Korea University Institute of International Education. Seoul, South Korea.

Yoon, J. Y. (2006a, May 26). One tenth of population aged over 65. *Korea Times*. Retrived online from LexisNexis database.

Yoon, J. Y. (2006b, May 9). Birthrate hit new low last year. *Korea Times*, p. 1.

Yoon, J. Y. (2006c, March 13). 14% of marriages international in 2005. *Korea Times*, p. 2.

In: South Korea
Editors: A. L. Hines and D. O. Mullins ISBN: 978-1-61942-377-0

Chapter 3

U.S.-SOUTH KOREA RELATIONS[1]

Mark E. Manyin, Emma Chanlett-Avery and Mary Beth Nikitin

SUMMARY

Since late 2008, relations between the United States and South Korea (known officially as the Republic of Korea, or ROK) have been arguably at their best state in decades. By the middle of 2010, in the view of many in the Obama Administration, South Korea had emerged as the United States' closest ally in East Asia.

Of all the issues on the bilateral agenda, Congress has the most direct role to play in the proposed Korea-U.S. Free Trade Agreement (KORUS FTA). Congressional approval is necessary for the agreement to go into effect. In early December 2010, the two sides announced they had agreed on modifications to the original agreement, which was signed in 2007. South Korea accepted a range of U.S. demands designed to help the U.S. auto industry and received some concessions in return. In the United States, the supplementary deal appears to have changed the minds of many groups and Members of Congress who previously had opposed the FTA, which is now

---

[1] This is an edited, reformatted and augmented version of the Congressional Research Service report, dated November 2010.

expected to be presented to the 112th Congress in 2011. If Congress approves the agreement, it would be the United States' second-largest FTA, after the North American Free Trade Agreement (NAFTA).

U.S.-South Korean coordination over policy towards North Korea has been particularly close. The Obama and Lee Administrations have adopted a medium-to-longer-term policy of "strategic patience" that involves four main elements: refusing to return to the Six-Party Talks without an assurance from North Korea that it would take "irreversible steps" to denuclearize; gradually attempting to alter China's strategic assessment of North Korea; using Pyongyang's provocations as opportunities to tighten sanctions against North Korean entities; and insisting that significant multilateral and U.S. talks with North Korea must be preceded by improvements in North-South Korean relations. Lee, in turn, has linked progress in many areas of North-South relations to progress in denuclearizing North Korea.

South Korea halted almost all remaining inter-Korean projects after the March 2010 sinking of the South Korean naval vessel, the *Cheonan*, an event the United States and South Korea have blamed on North Korea. Tensions with North Korea were further heightened by Pyongyang's late November 2010 shelling of a South Korean island, killing two South Korean soldiers and two civilians. The events further eroded the loose consensus that had prevailed in South Korea against openly discussing and planning for reunification in the short or medium term. While few South Koreans advocate actively trying to topple the Kim Jong-il regime, North Korea's actions have led many in the Lee government to view North Korea as much more of an immediate danger than previously thought. As a result, South Korea has adopted a new defense posture of "aggressive deterrence" that would involve a more significant military response to any North Korean attacks.

The United States maintains about 28,500 troops in the ROK. Since 2009, the two sides have accelerated steps to transform the U.S.-ROK alliance's primary purpose from one of defending against a North Korean attack to a regional and even global partnership. Washington and Seoul have announced a "Strategic Alliance 2015" plan to relocate U.S. troops on the Peninsula and boost ROK defense capabilities. Some Members of Congress have criticized the relocation plans.

Much of the current closeness between Seoul and Washington is due to President Lee. It is unclear how sustainable many of his policies will be, particularly into 2012, when South Koreans will elect a new president and a new legislature. Bilateral coordination will be particularly tested if South

Korea's left-of-center groups, which bitterly oppose much of Lee's agenda, retake the presidency and/or the National Assembly. This report will be updated periodically.

DEVELOPMENTS IN THE FIRST HALF OF 2011

New U.S. Ambassador Appointed

In June, President Obama announced his intent to nominate Sung Kim, chief representative to the Six-Party Talks over North Korea's nuclear program, to be the next Ambassador to South Korea. If confirmed by the Senate, Kim will be the first Korean American to hold the post. Kim, whose father was a South Korean government official, emigrated to the United States when he was seven, and became a U.S. citizen in the early 1980s.

The KORUS FTA

In 2007, the United States and South Korea signed the South Korea-U.S. Free Trade Agreement. If approved by both houses of Congress and the South Korean National Assembly, it would be the second-largest FTA by market size in which the United States participates (after the North American Free Trade Agreement, NAFTA). It would also be South Korea's second-largest FTA (after the Korea-European Union FTA, which went into effect on July 1, 2011).

As of early July 2011, the KORUS FTA remains poised for legislative action in both countries. In the United States, however, controversies over whether and how to link the FTA to other trade and economic measures have stalled the agreement. Throughout the winter and early spring of 2011, many Republican leaders pushed the Administration to submit the KORUS FTA together with the Colombia and Panama FTAs. In the spring of 2011, the Obama Administration announced that it had completed the technical procedures necessary to submit implementing legislation for the KORUS FTA—along with FTAs with Colombia and Panama—for congressional consideration. In May, the Administration announced it would not submit the three FTAs to Congress unless an agreement was reached on Trade Adjustment Assistance (TAA) programs, which provide aid for trade-affected workers, firms, farmers, and communities. A number of Republicans oppose reauthorizing TAA. In late June, the Obama Administration announced its intent to include TAA in the KORUS FTA's implementing bill and the Senate Finance Committee posted a draft implementing bill that included an extension of TAA programs. On July 7, the Senate Finance Committee held a "mock" markup of these bills and approved the combined KORUS FTA-TAA bill by a party-line 13-11 vote. The committee's 11 Republicans voted against the measure due to the inclusion of the TAA language. On the same day, the Republican-controlled House Ways and Means Committee voted 22-15 along party lines to approve a KORUS FTA bill without the TAA language. Many Democrats who support the KORUS FTA voted against the bill because the TAA language was excluded.

In South Korea, key members of the National Assembly indicated that they would likely delay moving forward on ratification of the KORUS FTA until the U.S. Congress took action. Additionally, in the late spring of 2011, Sohn Hak-kyu, the leader of the largest opposition party, the Democratic Party (DP), hardened his opposition to the agreement. Sohn has not indicated whether he will seek to boycott or physically block a vote, as his party has done in the past. Most observers think that the current National Assembly would approve the KORUS FTA, perhaps by a wide margin. (The ruling GNP—whose members appear to overwhelmingly favor the agreement—holds a comfortable majority in the National Assembly.) However, many warn that if a vote is not held until 2012, the fate of the KORUS FTA could become less certain due to the influence of 2012 electoral politics. In addition, President Lee's influence appears to be waning, and some GNP leaders have claimed to want to change the tone of politics in Seoul by, among other things, not ramming bills through the National Assembly.

North Korea Policy Coordination

For years, the Obama and Lee Administrations have essentially adopted a joint approach of "strategic patience" toward North Korea that involves four main elements: refusing to return to the Six-Party Talks over North Korea's nuclear program without a North Korean assurance that it would take "irreversible steps" to denuclearize; gradually attempting to alter China's strategic assessment of North Korea; using Pyongyang's provocations as opportunities to tighten sanctions against North Korean entities; and insisting that Six-Party Talks and/or U.S.-North Korean talks must be preceded by North-South Korean talks on denuclearization and improvements in North-South Korean relations. In early 2011, China backed the last of these principles, though it appears to have tried to use this stance to pressure South Korea (as well as the United States) to relax its conditions for holding talks with North Korea. Some have criticized the U.S. approach by saying that it effectively gives Seoul a "veto" over U.S. initiatives toward North Korea.

Throughout the spring and early summer of 2011, there were a number of press reports that Obama Administration officials also were encouraging the Lee government to soften South Korea's approach toward North Korea. If such speculation is accurate, it is not apparent from either the joint appearances by U.S. and South Korean officials or from the two countries' actions. In early 2011, Lee invited North Korea to participate in inter-Korean nuclear talks and in the 2012 Nuclear Security Summit, which will be held in Seoul. During the first half of 2011, South Korea also was involved in secret, high-level talks with North Korea that were disclosed by Pyongyang, apparently in an effort to embarrass Lee. The Lee government also has indicated its willingness to hold separate bilateral talks with North Korea on denuclearization and on overall inter-Korean relations. None of these initiatives necessarily represent a shift in South Korean policy, however. Indeed, South Korean officials have repeatedly stated their belief that progress in nuclear negotiations, including the Six-Party Talks, should be at least partially linked to North Korea's behavior toward South Korea—including some form of acknowledgement by Pyongyang of North Korea's role in various provocations in 2010 (discussed below).

One area of active U.S.-South Korean discussion, and perhaps debate, has been over whether one or both countries should provide food aid to North Korea, which has appealed for assistance. The Obama Administration is actively considering the North Korean request and in May dispatched an assessment team to North Korea to evaluate conditions there. South Korean officials indicated that their government would prefer that neither country provide large-scale assistance to North Korea unless Pyongyang changes its behavior.[1] On June 15, 2011, the House passed by voice vote an amendment to H.R. 2112, the FY20 12 Agriculture Appropriations Act, that would prohibit the Administration from using the primary U.S. food aid program to send food assistance to North Korea. The Senate has yet to act on H.R. 2112.

South Korea's New "Aggressive Deterrence" Military Posture

South Korean attitudes toward North Korea have hardened since 2010. In March of that year, a South Korean naval vessel, the *Cheonan*, sank. A multinational investigation team led by South Korea determined that the ship was sunk by a North Korean submarine. In November, North Korea shelled the South Korean island of Yeonpyeong Island, which lies across the inter-Korean disputed western sea border. The barrage killed four South Koreans (two marines and two civilians), wounded dozens, and destroyed or damaged scores of homes and other buildings

The provocations from North Korea, particularly the attack on Yeonpyeong Island, have introduced a new element of risk in the U.S.-South Korean alliance. In response to the attacks, the ROK military has strengthened its defense of its Northwest Islands and undertaken other structural changes to prepare for another possible provocation. South Korean President Lee stated that "war can be prevented and peace assured only when such provocations are met with a strong response. Fear of war is never helpful in preventing war ... the Armed Forces must respond relentlessly when they come under attack."[2] This posture, dubbed "aggressive deterrence," could increase the chance of conflict escalation on the Peninsula. U.S. defense officials insist, however, that the exceedingly close day-to-day coordination in the alliance ensures that U.S.-ROK communication would be strong in the event of a new contingency. General Walter Sharp, outgoing U.S. commander of the Combined Forces Command (CFC) in South Korea, confirmed to press outlets in July that the alliance had developed coordinated plans for countermeasures against any North Korean aggression.[3]

Issues Surrounding U.S. Troop Deployments in South Korea

In 2011, some Members of Congress have raised strong concerns with existing plans to relocate U.S. bases in South Korea and "normalize" the tours of U.S. troops there, including longer stays with family members accompanying them. In May 2011, Senators Carl Levin, John McCain, and James Webb issued a statement that urged a reconsideration of the existing plans for U.S. military presence in the Asia Pacific, including the current agreements in South Korea. A Government Accountability Office (GAO) report requested by members of the Senate Appropriations Committee released in May 2011 concluded that the Department of Defense had not demonstrated a "business case" to justify the tour normalization initiative, nor considered alternatives.[4] In June 2011, the Senate Armed Services Committee passed amendments to the 2012 Defense Authorization bill (S. 1253) that, if adopted, would prevent the obligation of any funds for tour normalization until further reviews of the plan are considered and a complete plan is provided to Congress. Critics of the Senators' call to overhaul existing plans say that such changes could restrict U.S. military capabilities and readiness as well as jeopardize hard-fought agreements designed to make U.S. presence more politically sustainable in South Korea.[5]

President Lee's Influence Waning?

In April 2011, President Lee's ruling Grand National Party (GNP) lost three of four national-level by-elections for seats in the unicameral National Assembly. Many interpreted the results as a sign that the opposition Democratic Party (DP) may perform well in next year's elections for South Korea's National Assembly (scheduled for April 2012) and/or presidency (scheduled for December 2012). The DP generally has been critical of President Lee's and President Obama's tough policy toward North Korea. Its members tend to be more willing to question various aspects of the U.S.-South Korea alliance, and most have opposed the Korea-U.S. Free Trade Agreement.

In reaction to the April 2011 election results, several GNP leaders resigned, and Lee replaced several members of his Cabinet. Many have observed that Lee's clout over the GNP has declined markedly due to the elections and his "lame duck" status.[6] A number of GNP members have declared their candidacy for the presidency. Thus far, the front-runner according to virtually all polls is an undeclared candidate, Ms. Park Geun-hye, whom Lee narrowly defeated in the GNP primary in 2007. The GNP continues to be divided between pro-Lee and pro-Park camps. Until the spring of 2011, the pro-Lee factions generally were ascendant.

In early July 2011, a new GNP leadership team was selected through a combination of GNP members' votes and a random telephone survey of South Korean citizens. Many analysts interpreted the results as further evidence of Lee's declining clout. The top two vote-getters - including the new GNP chairman, Hong Chun-pyo - are seen as closely tied to Park Geun-hye. Three of the five members chosen for the leadership council are in their 40s, making the GNP's current leadership team one of the youngest in memory.

Lee's apparently diminished clout likely will make it difficult for him to undertake major new or controversial initiatives. Most major issues in U.S.-South Korean relations are likely to be insulated from Lee's political fortunes, for at least two reasons: (1) the institutional dominance of South Korea's presidency; and (2) the GNP's continued control over the National Assembly. The link between South Korean politics and U.S. interests could become more direct, however, if new sources of bilateral controversy flare up or if the "progressive" camp, led by the DP, should win a majority in the April 2012 National Assembly elections.

Reports of Dumping of Agent Orange at U.S. Bases

In the spring of 2011, several U.S. veterans stated to U.S. news organizations that during the 1960s and 1970s they been ordered to bury chemicals, including the defoliant "Agent Orange" dioxin, on U.S. military bases in South Korea. United States Forces Korea (USFK) and South Korea's Ministry of the Environment began investigating and testing samples at the sites, some of which are on land that has been returned to South Korea, to see if there are signs of contamination. As of early July 2011, no major health problems appear to have been linked to the sites in question. The results of the first round of testing are expected to be completed in July 2011. In the weeks after the revelations, USFK officials won praise from across the South Korean political spectrum for their speed, transparency, and humbleness in responding. However, the issue could become an irritant in bilateral relations if many South Koreans begin to suspect a cover-up or a violation of U.S.-South Korean agreements.

South Korea's Pyeongchang Chosen to Host 2018 Winter Olympics

In a sign of South Korea's continued emergence as a global player, International Olympic Committee (IOC) delegates in early July 2011 voted overwhelmingly to award the 2018 Olympics to Pyeongchang, a city of 40,000 located about 110 miles east of Seoul. Pyeongchang had lost in the final round of two previous bids, in 2003 (for the 2010 Games, which were awarded to Vancouver) and in 2007 (for the 2014 Games, which will be held in Sochi, Russia). South Korea's bids at the time were criticized for the lack of world-class facilities in Pyeongchang. In response, the South Korean government and various companies cooperated to spend billions of dollars in new facilities and infrastructure in and around the city. According to one report, between 2011 and 2018 the government plans to spend roughly 20 trillion won (approximately $19 billion), including around $3 billion for a high-speed rail connection to Seoul.[7]

In its two previous Winter Games bids, South Korea's proposals reportedly emphasized the Olympics' potential to help ease tensions between North and South Korea. In contrast, the 2018 bid—under the slogan of "New Horizons"—stressed Pyeongchang's ambitions to become a new regional winter sports center. After the result was announced, IOC President Jacques Rogge said that among the reasons for Pyeongchang's selection were that the bid "enjoys massive support from the government and the public," and that "the South Korean project will leave a tremendous legacy as ... a new winter sports hub in Asia."[8]

Overview

While the U.S.-South Korea relationship is highly complex and multifaceted, five factors arguably drive the scope and state of U.S.-South Korea relations:

- the challenges posed by North Korea, particularly its weapons of mass destruction programs and perceptions in Washington and Seoul of whether the Kim regime poses a threat, through its belligerence and/or the risk of its collapse;
- the growing desire of South Korean leaders to use the country's middle power status to play a larger regional and, more recently, global role;
- increasingly, China's rising influence in Northeast Asia, which has become an integral consideration in many aspects of U.S.-South Korea strategic and (to a lesser extent) economic policymaking;
- South Korea's transformation into one of the world's leading economies—with a very strong export-oriented industrial base—which has led to an expansion of trade disputes and helped drive the two countries' decision to sign a free trade agreement; and
- South Korea's continued democratization, which has raised the importance of public opinion in Seoul's foreign policy.

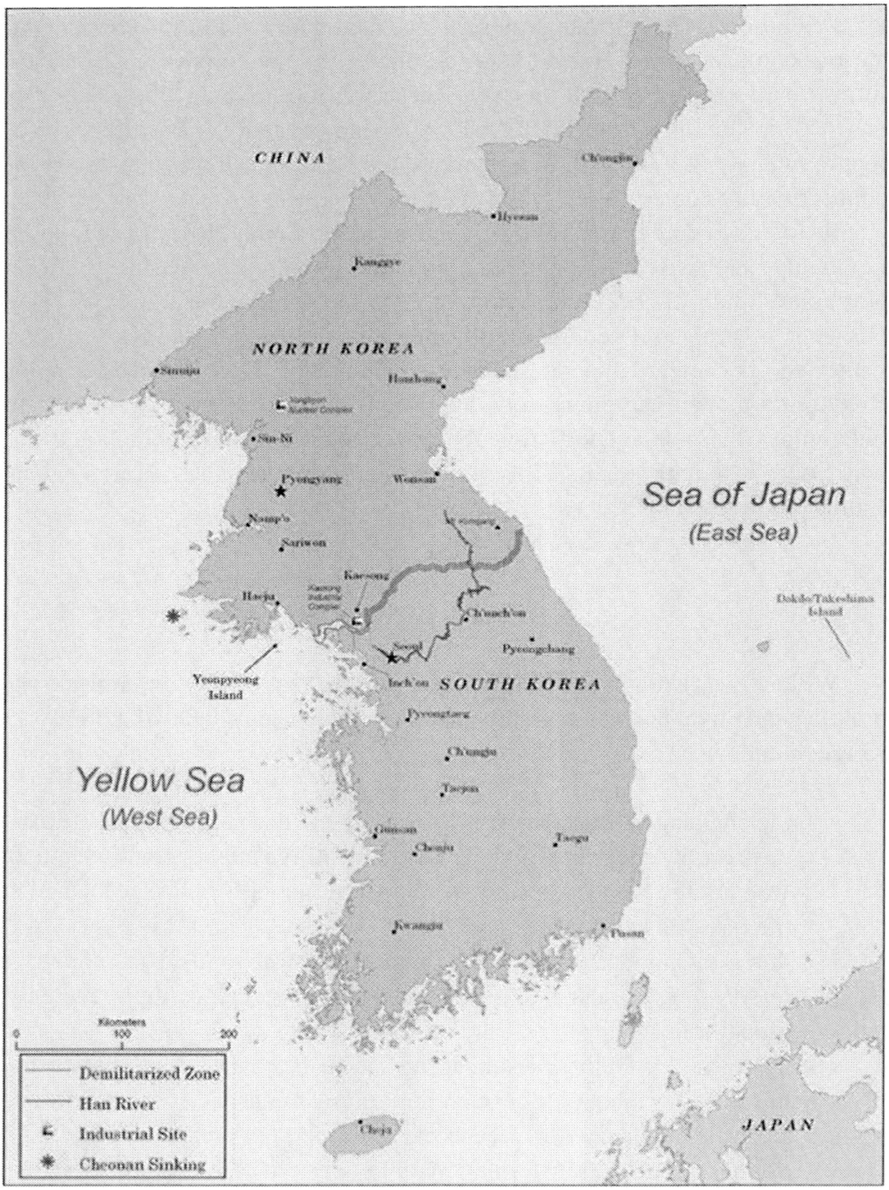

Source: Prepared by CRS based on ESRI Data and Maps 9.3.1; IHS World Data.

Figure 1. Map of the Korean Peninsula.

Additionally, while people-to-people ties generally do not directly affect matters of "high" politics in bilateral relations, the presence of over 1.2 million Korean Americans and the hundreds of thousands of trips taken annually between the two countries has helped cement the two countries together.[9]

Since late 2008, relations between the United States and South Korea have been arguably at their best state in nearly a decade, if not ever. Coordination over North Korea policy has been particularly close, with one high-level official in late 2009 describing the two countries as being "not just on the same page, but on the same paragraph."[10] At a summit in June 2009, the two parties signed a "Joint Vision" statement that foresees the transformation of the alliance's purpose from one of primarily defending against a North Korean attack to a regional and even global alliance, in which Washington and Seoul cooperate on a myriad of issues, including climate change, energy security, terrorism, economic development, and human rights promotion, as well as peacekeeping and the stabilization of post-conflict situations. Reflecting this evolution, in a June 2010 meeting with President Lee, President Obama referred to the alliance as "the lynchpin" for security in the Pacific region. This statement stirred some degree of anxiety in Tokyo; Japan has traditionally considered itself to be the most significant U.S. partner in the region.

Much of this closeness is due to the policies of President Lee, including his determination after assuming office to improve Seoul's relations with Washington. However, it is unclear how much domestic support exists for some of President Lee's policies. On North Korea, for instance, the United States and South Korea often have different priorities, with many if not most South Koreans generally putting more emphasis on regional stability than on deterring nuclear proliferation, the top U.S. priority. Currently, these differences have been masked by North Korea's general belligerence since early 2009 and to a large extent negated by President Lee's consistent stance that progress on the nuclear issue is a prerequisite for improvements in many areas of North-South relations. Also, President Lee's enthusiastic support for expanding the role of the U.S.-ROK alliance beyond the Korean Peninsula has come under domestic criticism.

Moreover, while large majorities of South Koreans say they value the U.S.-ROK alliance, many South Koreans are resentful of U.S. influence and chafe when they feel their leaders offer too many concessions to the United States. This is particularly the case among Korea's left-of-center, or "progressive" groups, who bitterly oppose much of President Lee's policy agenda and his governing style.

Thus, it is unclear how sustainable the current bilateral intimacy is likely to be, particularly beyond 2011. South Korea's legislative and presidential elections in 2012 could erode some of the momentum established under Lee. Bilateral coordination will be particularly tested if South Korea's progressives retake the presidential office (called the Blue House) and/or the National Assembly.

Historical Background

The United States and South Korea have been allies since the United States intervened on the Korean Peninsula in 1950 and fought to repel a North Korean takeover of South Korea. Over 33,000 U.S. troops were killed and over 100,000 were wounded during the three-year conflict. In 1954, a year after the parties to the conflict signed an armistice agreement, the United States and South Korea signed a Mutual Defense Treaty, which provides that if either party is attacked by a third country, the other party will act to meet the common danger. The United States maintains about 28,500 troops in the ROK to supplement the 650,000-strong South Korean armed forces. South Korea deployed troops to support the U.S.-led military campaign in Vietnam. South Korea subsequently has assisted U.S. deployments in other conflicts, most recently by deploying over 3,000 troops to play a non-combat role in Iraq and over 300 non-combat troops to Afghanistan.

Beginning in the 1960s, rapid economic growth propelled South Korea into the ranks of the world's largest industrialized countries. For over a decade, South Korea has been one of the United States' largest trading partners. Economic growth also has helped transform the ROK into a mid-level regional power that can influence U.S. policy in Northeast Asia, particularly the United States' approach toward North Korea.

North Korea in U.S.-ROK Relations

Policy Coordination

Dealing with North Korea is the dominant strategic element of the U.S.-South Korean relationship. Since breakdown of the Six-Party Talks in late 2008 and North Korea's second nuclear test in May 2009, coordination over North Korea policy has been remarkably close. South Korea's growing economic, diplomatic, and military power has given Seoul a much more direct and prominent role in Washington's planning and thinking about how to deal with Pyongyang. One indicator of South Korea's centrality to diplomacy over North Korea is that no successful round of the Six-Party nuclear talks has taken place when inter-Korean relations have been poor.

For much of the 2000s, policy coordination between the United States and South Korea was difficult, sometimes extremely so, because the countries' policies toward Pyongyang were often out-of-synch, and at times and in many ways contradictory. Presidents Kim Dae-jung (1998- 2003) and Roh Moo-hyun (2003-2008) pursued a "sunshine policy" of largely unconditional engagement with North Korea that clashed with the harder policy line pursued by the Bush Administration until late 2006. President Roh, who was elected in part because of his embrace of massive anti-American protests that ensued after a U.S. military vehicle killed two Korean schoolgirls in 2002, also alarmed U.S. policymakers by speaking of a desire that South Korea should play a "balancing" role among China, the United States, and Japan in Northeast Asia. Despite this, under Roh's tenure, South Korea deployed over 3,000 non-combat troops to Iraq - the third-largest contingent in the international coalition—and the two sides initiated and signed the KORUS FTA. Although relations between the two capitals improved dramatically after President Lee Myung-bak's 2008 inauguration, his tougher stance toward North Korea was not always aligned with the late Bush Administration's push for a nuclear deal with North Korea.

Coordination over the Cheonan Sinking

The two Administrations' closeness has been both confirmed and cemented by their coordinated reaction to the March 2010 sinking of a South Korean naval vessel, the *Cheonan*. Forty-six South Korean sailors died in the incident. A multinational investigation team led by South Korea determined that the ship was sunk by a North Korean submarine.[11] In the wake of the sinking, U.S.-South Korean cooperation was underscored by a series of military exercises in the waters surrounding the peninsula, as well as symbolic gestures such as the joint visit of Secretary of State Clinton and Secretary of Defense Gates to the Demilitarized Zone (DMZ). During the visit, a new set of unilateral U.S. sanctions targeting North Korea were announced.[12]

New Revelations of North Korea's Uranium Enrichment Capabilities[13]

In November 2010, the relative quietude in North Korea's relations with South Korea and the United States that had predominated in the months after the *Cheonan* sinking was shattered by two events. First, North Korea showed Dr. Siegfried Hecker, the former head of the U.S. Los Alamos National Laboratory, a new "ultra-modern" uranium enrichment facility with 2,000 centrifuges that the North Koreans said is producing low enriched uranium destined for fuel for a new light-water nuclear reactor that is under construction. The revelation confirmed longstanding fears that North Korea has been developing an alternative, uranium-based nuclear program to complement or replace its existing plutonium-based facilities. Although Dr. Hecker has said that the centrifuge plant and the new reactor appear to be designed primarily for civilian nuclear power, the uranium facilities could also be used to produce fissile material suitable for nuclear weapons.[14]

North Korea's Artillery Attack Against South Korea

Second, on November 23, only days after the uranium revelations, North Korean artillery units fired over 150 shells on to and around Yeonpyeong Island, across the North-South disputed western sea border. North Korea claimed that the South Korean military had fired first, during routine U.S.-ROK exercises in the area. According to one report, about half the North Korean shells hit the island. The barrage killed four South Koreans (two marines and two civilians), wounded dozens, and destroyed or damaged scores of homes and other buildings.[15] It was North Korea's first direct artillery attack on ROK territory since the 1950-1953 Korean War. South Korea responded by shooting 80 shells at North Korea. An official North Korean media outlet later said that the South Korean civilian deaths were "regrettable."[16]

The attacks prompted a number of responses:

- South Korea and the United States held large-scale naval exercises in the Yellow Sea area with the USS *George Washington* aircraft carrier strike group. After the *Cheonan* sinking, the U.S. and South Korea had refrained from staging exercises in the Yellow Sea area, after China had warned of its sensitivity to military activities there.
- In a nationally televised speech, Lee announced that South Korea would no longer hold back on retaliating for North Korean provocations. President Lee and the South Korean military have come under strong domestic criticism for what was widely perceived as faulty military preparation and a delayed counterattack, prompting the

defense minister to resign. His successor stated that if attacked in the future, South Korea would consider using its air force to strike back in North Korean territory.[17]

- China, after consulting widely among the other negotiating parties, proposed a meeting of participants in the Six-Party Talks to stabilize the situation. South Korea, the United States, and Japan rejected such a move, saying that it would only reward North Korea's attack and was premature without signs that North Korea would change its behavior.
- Instead, the three countries stepped up trilateral cooperation and called on China to do more to pressure North Korea. Secretary of State Clinton met in Washington, DC, with the South Korean and Japanese foreign ministers, where the three condemned North Korea's attack, affirmed their solidarity in dealing with North Korea, and discussed cooperation on a range of regional and global issues. Relatedly, for the first time, South Korea sent military observers to a U.S. and Japanese joint military exercise. 1[8]

INTER-KOREAN RELATIONS

Relations between the two Koreas have deteriorated markedly since Lee's February 2008 inauguration. After 10 years of Seoul's "sunshine" policy of largely unconditioned reconciliation with North Korea, the Lee government entered office insisting on more reciprocity from and conditionality toward Pyongyang. Most importantly, the Lee government announced that it would review the initiation of new large-scale inter-Korean projects agreed to before Lee took office, and that implementation would be linked to progress in denuclearizing North Korea. In another reversal of his predecessors' policies, Lee's government has been openly critical of human rights conditions in North Korea. His administration also offered to continue humanitarian assistance—provided North Korea first requests such aid—and indicated that existing inter-Korean projects would be continued.

North Korea reacted to Lee's overall approach by unleashing a wave of invective against Lee and adopting a more hostile stance toward official inter-Korean activities. Inter-Korean relations have steadily worsened since then, to the point that by September 2010, nearly all of the inter-Korean meetings, hotlines, tours, exchanges, and other programs that had been established during the "sunshine" period have been suspended or severely curtailed.[19]

Whether it is a coincidence or a cause, since Lee's inauguration North Korea has behaved more provocatively, with each provocation leading South Korea to take a harder line, which in turn has led North Korea to respond.[20]

The most dramatic playing out of this dynamic occurred in the spring of 2010. In response to the sinking of the *Cheonan*, South Korea curtailed nearly all forms of North-South interaction, including all business transactions except for those associated with the inter-Korean industrial park in the North Korean city of Kaesong. Despite periodic restrictions, the Kaesong Complex continues to operate and has expanded slightly under Lee.[21]

In August 2010 Lee publicly floated the idea of creating a "reunification tax" that would help prepare South Korea for a future reuniting of the two Koreas. Previously, a loose consensus had prevailed in South Korea against openly discussing and planning for reunification in the short or medium term, because of fears of provoking Pyongyang and of the fiscal costs of absorbing the impoverished North. While few South Koreans advocate for actively trying to topple the Kim regime, the reunification tax proposal indicates how the *Cheonan* sinking has led many in the Lee government to view North Korea as more much more of an immediate danger than previously thought.

Polls of South Korean attitudes show widespread and increasing anger toward and concern about North Korea. Opinion toward North Korea hardened after the shelling of Yeonpyeong Island, with fewer Koreans expressing support for a return to the largely unconditional engagement with North Korea that occurred during the "sunshine policy" era. However, polls also show continued ambivalence toward Lee's approach and a desire among many, if not most, South Koreans for their government to show more flexibility toward Pyongyang.

In July 2009, South Korea began circulating to other governments and key private sector groups a proposal for a $40 billion multilateral aid fund and development strategy that would help North Korea if Pyongyang denuclearized. According to the details provided by various media outlets, the proposal appears to be a continuation of Lee's "3,000 Policy" pledge during the 2007 presidential campaign to help raise North Korea's per capita income to $3,000 over the next 10 years.[22] The proposal also appears to complement the "comprehensive" package the Obama Administration has indicated could be forthcoming if North Korea took positive steps on the nuclear front.

South Korea's Regional Relations

Looking at their surrounding neighborhood, South Koreans sometimes refer to themselves as a "shrimp among whales." South Korea's relations with China and Japan, especially the latter, are fraught with ambivalence, combining interdependence and rivalry. Despite these difficulties, trilateral cooperation among the three capitals has increased over the past decade, particularly in the aftermath of the 2008 global financial crisis. Since 2008, leaders of the three countries have met annually in standalone summits and in 2010 agreed to undertake an official study of a trilateral FTA and to establish a secretariat in Seoul.[23]

Growing South Korea-Japan Cooperation

A cooperative relationship between South Korea and Japan, both U.S. treaty allies, and among the three countries is in U.S. interests because it arguably enhances regional stability, helps coordination over North Korea policy, and boosts each country's ability to deal with the strategic challenges posed by China's rise. However, despite increased cooperation, closeness, and interdependence between the South Korean and Japanese governments, people, and businesses over the past decade, mistrust on historical and territorial issues continues to linger. South Korea and Japan have competing claims to the small Dokdo/Takeshima islets in the Sea of Japan (called the East Sea by Koreans), and most South Koreans complain that Japan has not adequately acknowledged its history of aggression against Korea. For more than three generations beginning in the late 19th century, Japan intervened directly in Korean affairs, culminating in the annexation of the Korean peninsula in 1910. Over the next 35 years, Imperial Japan all but attempted to wipe out Korean culture.[24]

President Lee came into office seeking to improve official South Korea-Japan relations, which had deteriorated markedly during President Roh's term. Under Lee, and throughout a succession of Japanese leaders, Cabinet and head-of-state meetings, including reciprocal visits, have become more routine. Cemented for the first time in years by a common strategic outlook on North Korea, trilateral South Korea-U.S.-Japan coordination over North Korea policy has been particularly close since the beginning of 2009 and has become even tighter since the sinking of the Cheonan. People-to-people ties have blossomed, with tens of thousands of Japanese and Koreans traveling to the other country every day. Tens of thousands of South Koreans, including some victims of Japan's colonial period, donated funds to Japan after the March 11 earthquake and tsunami off the coast of northeastern Japan. The South Korean and Japanese militaries also have stepped up their cooperation. Lee has given less public emphasis to flare-ups over history and the Dokdo/Takeshima territorial dispute. He also welcomed the most recent Japanese apology for its history of aggression, from Prime Minister Naoto Kan in August 2010, that recognized the 100th anniversary of Japan's annexation. Many observers said that the apology, along with Kan's move to return thousands of antiquities taken from Korea during the occupation, were major reasons South Korean protests marking the anniversary were much smaller and less virulent than had been expected.

However, South Koreans' interest in forming significant new institutional arrangements with Japan is dampened by three factors. First, continued suspicions of Japan among the South Korean population place political limitations on how far and how fast Korean leaders can improve relations. Second, continued disagreements over Dokdo/Takeshima's sovereignty continue to weigh down the relationship. A key to this issue will be whether such disputes are contained or spill over into other areas of the relationship. Third, unlike Japan, South Korea generally does not view China as an existential challenge and territorial threat. South Korea also needs Chinese cooperation on North Korea. Accordingly, Korean leaders tend to be much more wary of taking steps that will alarm China. A factor that could change this calculation is if China is seen as enabling North Korean aggression, as most South Korean leaders believe was the case after the Yeonpyeong Island shelling.

Two indicators to watch over the coming months in South Korea-Japan relations are (1) whether the two countries can restart and complete free trade agreement negotiations that have been stalled since 2004, and (2) whether they can complete negotiations over an information sharing and an Acquisition and Cross-Servicing Agreement (ACSA), both of which would facilitate greater cooperation and coordination between the two countries' militaries. In March 2011, a Japanese Ministry of Education panel announced that middle school history textbooks must state that Dokdo/Takeshima is Japanese territory. South Koreans protested. Although the response appears to have been more muted than in the past, the ACSA and military information sharing talks have not been held since then. Another flare-up of the sovereignty dispute is expected to come in August, when Japan's Defense Ministry issues its annual white paper.

South Korea-China Relations

China's rise influences virtually all aspects of South Korean foreign and economic policy. North Korea's growing economic and diplomatic dependence on China since the early 2000s has meant that South Korea must increasingly factor Beijing's actions and intentions into its North Korea policy. China's influence over North Korea has tended to manifest itself in two ways in Seoul. On the one hand, most South Korean officials worry that North Korea, particularly its northern provinces, are drifting into China's orbit. Kim Jong-il has made an unprecedented three trips to China in the 2010-2011 time period, and the two countries have greatly expanded economic cooperation between provinces straddling their border. For those on the political left in South Korea, this has been an argument against Lee's harder line stance toward inter-Korean relations, which they say has eroded much of South Korea's influence over North Korea. On the other hand, China's continued support for North Korea, particularly its month-long delay in expressing public regret over the *Cheonan's* sinking and its perceived backing of Pyongyang after the Yeonpyeong Island shelling, has angered many South Koreans, particularly conservatives. Many South Korean conservatives also express concern that their Chinese counterparts have been unwilling to discuss plans for dealing with various contingencies involving instability in North Korea. Furthermore, South Koreans' concerns about China's rise have been heightened by China's increased assertiveness around East Asia in recent years, particularly its vocal opposition in 2010 to U.S.- South Korean naval exercises in the Yellow Sea.

Since China's 2001 entry into the World Trade Organization, it has emerged as South Korea's most important economic partner. Over 20% of South Korea's total trade is with China, and for years China has been the number one location for South Korean firms' foreign direct investment.[25] Yet, even as China is an important source of South Korean economic growth, it also looms large as an economic competitor. Indeed, fears of increased competition with Chinese enterprises has been an important motivator for South Korea's push to negotiate a series of free trade agreements around the globe.

Security Relations and the U.S.-ROK Alliance

The United States and South Korea are allies under the 1953 Mutual Defense Treaty. Under the agreement, U.S. military personnel have maintained a continuous presence on the peninsula since the conclusion of the Korean War and are committed to help South Korea defend itself, particularly against any aggression from the North. South Korea is included under the U.S. "nuclear umbrella," also known as "extended deterrence" that applies to other non-nuclear U.S. allies as well.

The U.S.-ROK alliance has enjoyed a significant boost in recent years after a period of strain under the George W. Bush and Roh Moo-hyun Administrations. Even before the *Cheonan* sinking, South Korea's willingness to send troops to Afghanistan and increasing defense expenditures reinforced the sense that the alliance is flourishing. Emblematic of the close ties, the South Korean and U.S. foreign and defense ministers held their first ever "2+2" meeting in July 2010, which featured a visit to the Demilitarized Zone (DMZ) by Secretary of State Clinton and Secretary of Defense Gates. The historic meeting both commemorated the 60th anniversary of the Korean War and demonstrated the enduring strength of the alliance. The massive joint military exercises held immediately after the meeting, featuring a U.S. aircraft carrier and F-22 aircraft, signaled to North Korea and others that the American commitment to Korea remains strong.

Budgetary and Operational Challenges

Despite these indicators of strength, the alliance faces a host of significant challenges in the months and years ahead. Delays and increasing price tags have slowed the implementation of agreements to reduce and relocate the U.S. troop presence in South Korea. Differences over burden sharing remain, but analysts note that these issues tend to be prevalent in all alliance relationships. Although the political atmospherics of the alliance have been outstanding, defense analysts note that the Lee Administration has slowed significantly the defense budget increases planned under the earlier Roh Administration.

U.S. Alliance and ROK Defense Reform Plans

Current security developments are taking place in the context of several concurrent defense schemes. The June 2009 Obama-Lee summit produced the broadly conceived "**Joint Vision for the Alliance**," which promised to enhance and globalize future defense cooperation. After the decision to delay the Opcon transfer, the operational "**Strategic Alliance 2015**" roadmap (announced in September 2010) outlines the new transition, including ROK capabilities and U.S. troop relocation and tour normalization. The U.S. military is also undergoing a broad transformation of its forces in the region; the 8th Army is moving toward becoming a warfighting headquarters that can deploy to other areas of the world while still serving as a deterrent to any possible aggression from North Korea.[26]

Meanwhile, South Korea's **Defense Reform 2020** bill passed by the National Assembly in 2006 remains officially in effect. The plan lays out a 15-year, 621 trillion *won* (about $550 million) investment that aims to reduce the number of ROK troops while developing a high-tech force and strengthening the Joint Chief of Staff system. In addition, an evolving plan known as "**Defense Reformation Plan 307**," intends to enhance collaboration among the ROK military branches. Driven by the North Korean provocations in 2010, the new approach calls for a more flexible posture to respond to future attacks, as opposed to the "total war" scenario that has driven much of Seoul's defense planning in the past.

Defense Reform 2020 calls for defense budget increases of 9.9% each year, but the Lee Administration reduced the increase to 3.6% for FY2010, citing economic pressures.[27] Following the *Cheonan* sinking and amid calls for improved capabilities to counter the North, however, the Defense Ministry requested a budget increase for funds toward the acquisition of surveillance aircraft to monitor the North's unconventional threat and to improve weapons systems on ROK islands in the Yellow Sea.[28] The 2011 defense budget was approved at a 6.2% increase over the 2010 budget.[29]

The Relocation of U.S. Forces Korea (USFK)

In 2004, Secretary of Defense Donald Rumsfeld authorized a realignment program to reduce and relocate U.S. forces in South Korea. Under the Rumsfeld program, the Pentagon withdrew a 3,600-person combat brigade from the Second Division and sent it to Iraq. The Rumsfeld plan called for the

U.S. troop level in South Korea to fall from 37,000 to 25,000 by September 2008. However, in 2008, Secretary of Defense Gates halted the withdrawals at the level of 28,500.

The U.S. Forces Korea (USFK) relocation plan has two elements. The first envisages the transfer of a large percentage of the 9,000 U.S. military personnel at the U.S. Yongsan base in Seoul to U.S. Army Garrison (USAG) Humphreys, which is located near the city of Pyeongtaek some 40 miles south of Seoul. The second element involves the withdrawal of about 10,000 troops of the Second Infantry Division from the demilitarized zone and their relocation to areas south of the Han River (which runs through Seoul). The end result will be that USFK's sites will decline from the 104 it maintained in 2002, to 48. The bulk of U.S. forces will be clustered in the two primary "hubs" of Osan Air Base/USAG Humphreys and USAG Daegu that contain five "enduring sites" (Osan Air Base, USAG Humphreys, US AG Daegu, Chinhae Naval Base, and Kunsan Air Base). A new joint warrior training center, north of Seoul, will be opened.[30]

The relocations to Pyeongtaek originally were scheduled for completion in 2008, but have been postponed several times because of the slow construction of new facilities at Pyongtaek and South Korean protests of financial difficulties in paying the ROK share of the relocation costs. The original cost estimate was over $10 billion; South Korea was to contribute $4 billion of this. Estimates in 2010 placed the costs over $13 billion. In congressional testimony in September 2010, U.S. officials demurred from providing a final figure on the cost of the move, but confirmed that the South Koreans were paying more than the original $4 billion.[31] U.S.-ROK discussions in 2009 reportedly indicated that the relocations to Pyeongtaek will not take place until 2015 or 2016. Some individuals involved and familiar with the move speculate that it will not be completed until 2020.

Tour Normalization

Another complicating factor in the development of the Yongsan Relocation Plan is the announcement by the Pentagon in 2008 that U.S. military families, for the first time, would be allowed to join U.S. military personnel in South Korea. Prior to this change, most U.S. troops in South Korea served one-year unaccompanied assignments. The goal is to phase out one-year unaccompanied tours in South Korea, replacing them with 36-month accompanied or 24-month unaccompanied tours. Eventually, the "normalization" of tours is estimated to increase the size of the U.S. military

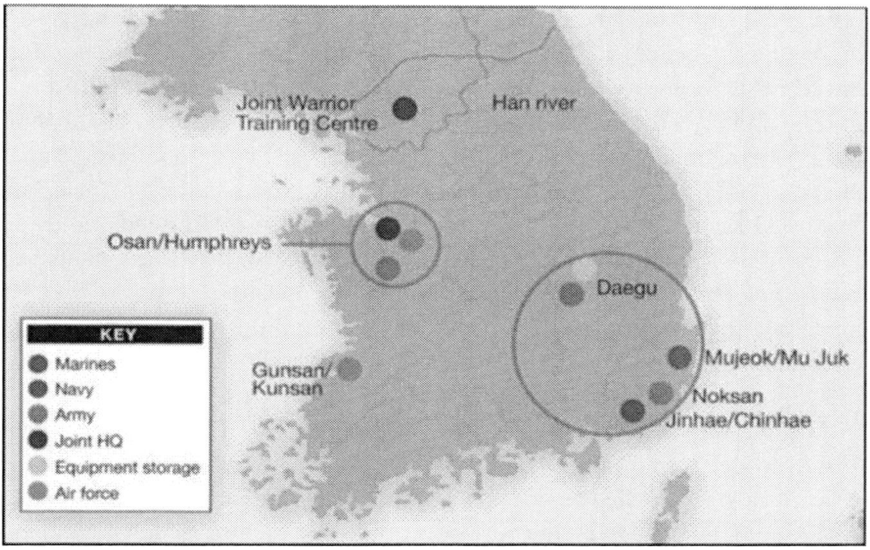

Source: *Jane's Sentinel Security Assessment - China And Northeast Asia*, date posted April 15, 2010.

Figure 2. USFK Bases After Realignment Plan is Implemented.

community at Osan/Humphries near Pyongtaek to over 50,000. Members of Congress have raised concerns about the cost of the normalization initiative and requested a review of the plan.

Cost Sharing

Under a Special Measures Agreement reached in 2009, South Korea's direct financial contribution for U.S. troops in South Korea in 2011 will be 812.5 billion *won* (about $743 million). This is about 42% of the total cost of maintaining U.S. forces in South Korea. In recent U.S.-R.O.K. military negotiations, Pentagon officials called for South Korea to increase its share to at least 50%. Under the 2009 agreement, South Korea's share of the cost is to increase until 2013 in accord with the rate of inflation but no more than 4% annually.

Opcon Transfer

The United States has agreed with Seoul to turn over the wartime command of Korean troops later this decade. Under the current arrangement, which is a legacy of U.S. involvement in the 1950-1953 Korean War, South

Korea's soldiers would be under the command of U.S. forces if there were a war on the peninsula. In 2007, Secretary Rumsfeld accepted a proposal by then- South Korean President Roh Moo-hyun to set up separate South Korean and U.S. military commands by April 2012. A U.S.-R.O.K. operational control (Opcon) agreement will dismantle the U.S.-R.O.K. Combined Forces Command (CFC), which has been headed by the U.S. commander in Korea. Separate U.S. and R.O.K. military commands will be established. In accord with the plan a new U.S. Korea Command (KORCOM) will be established. Under the Opcon agreement, a Military Cooperation Center will be responsible for planning military operations, joint military exercises, logistics support, and intelligence exchanges, and assisting in the operation of the communication, command, control, and computer systems.

At their June 2010 summit, Presidents Obama and Lee announced their decision to delay the transfer of Opcon by three years, until 2015. Although the decision was couched as sending a strong signal to North Korea following the sinking of the *Cheonan*, the agreement followed months of debate in Seoul and Washington about the timing of the transfer. Many South Korean and U.S. experts questioned whether the South Korean military possesses the capabilities—such as a joint command and control system, sufficient transport planes, and amphibious sea lift vessels—to operate effectively as its own command by the original transfer date of 2012. U.S. officials stress, however, that the transfer was militarily on track before the political decision to postpone. Opposition to the transfer in some quarters in Seoul may reflect a traditional fear of abandonment by the U.S. military.

With the decision made, U.S. commanders are arguing that the three-year delay will allow the alliance to synchronize more thoroughly all the moving parts of the arrangement, including the relocation of U.S. troops.[32] The Strategic Alliance 2015 plan envisages measures such as upgrading South Korean defense capabilities (such as ground operations command), improving and recalibrating USFK and South Korean command and control systems, and better aligning military exercises to meet the new asymmetrical challenges posed by North Korea.

The "Strategic Flexibility" of USFK

In 2007 and 2008, U.S. commanders in South Korea stated that the future U.S. role in the defense of South Korea would be mainly an air force and naval role. The ROK armed forces today total 681,000 troops, with nearly 550,000 of them in the Army and around 65,000 each in the Air Force and Navy. Since 2004, the U.S. Air Force has increased its strength in South Korea through the regular rotation into South Korea of advanced strike aircraft. These rotations are not a permanent presence, but the aircraft often remain in South Korea for weeks and sometimes months for training.

Since the early 2000s, U.S. military officials have expressed a desire to deploy some U.S. forces in South Korea to areas of international conflicts under a doctrine of "strategic flexibility." The South Korean government of Roh Moo-hyun resisted this idea, largely for fear it might entangle South Korea in a possible conflict between the United States and China. In the mid-2000s, the two governments reached an agreement in which South Korea recognized the United States' intention to be able to deploy its forces off the Peninsula, while the United States in turn recognized that the troops' return to South Korea would be subject to discussion. Among other elements, the compromise seems to imply that in an off-Peninsula contingency, U.S. forces might deploy but not operate from South Korea.

South Korean Defense Industry and Purchases of U.S. Weapons

South Korea is a major purchaser of U.S. weapons, buying $966.9 million worth of U.S. arms in FY20 10. The country is regularly among the top customers for Foreign Military Sales (FMS).[33] Although South Korea generally buys the majority of its weapons from the United States, European defense companies also compete for contracts; Korea is an attractive market because of its rising defense expenditures. Recently, Boeing won the first two phases of South Korea's fighter modernization program and Seoul has also indicated interest in Lockheed Martin's F-35 Joint Strike Fighter.[34] South Korea's defense ministry has said that it will prioritize its defense systems against North Korea's missile and nuclear threats, including Aegis combat destroyers, missile interceptors, and early warning radars.[35] In response to recent attacks, Seoul has deployed precision-guided missiles near the DMZ[36] and is currently developing a next generation multiple launch rocket system to be placed near the Northern Limit Line.[37]

Korea's Defense Reform 2020 legislation emphasizes the development of indigenous capabilities by increasing the percentage of funds allocated to defense research and development (R&D).[38] South Korea competes internationally in the armored vehicle, shipbuilding, and aerospace industries. Of particular note is the T-50 Golden Eagle, a trainer and light fighter aircraft developed in conjunction with Lockheed Martin.[39]

The 110th Congress passed legislation that upgraded South Korea's status as an arms purchaser from a Major Non-NATO Ally to the NATO Plus Three category (P.L. 110-429), which changed the classification to NATO Plus Four.

This upgrade establishes a higher dollar threshold for the requirement that the U.S. executive branch notify Congress of pending arms sales to South Korea, from $14 million to $25 million. Congress has 15 days to consider the sale, and may take legislative steps to block the sale compared to 50 days for Major Non-NATO Allies.

South Korea's Deployment to Afghanistan

After withdrawing its initial deployment of military personnel to Afghanistan in 2007, South Korea sent a second deployment, consisting of troops and civilian workers who are staffing a Provincial Reconstruction Team (PRT) in Parwan Province, located north of Kabul.[40] In February 2010, the National Assembly approved and funded the deployment of over 320 Army personnel and 40 police officers to protect 100 Korean civilian reconstruction workers for a two-year mission. The first soldiers arrived in June 2010 and are scheduled to stay until the end of 2012. Increasing numbers of attacks on Korean facilities, coupled with the Obama Administration decision to begin troop withdrawal in summer 2011, have raised questions about an early return of some ROK personnel. According to some South Korean press reports, the ROK government is considering an earlier withdrawal.

ECONOMIC RELATIONS

South Korea and the United States are major economic partners. In 2010, two-way trade between the two countries totaled over $86 billion (see Table 1), making South Korea the United States' seventh-largest trading partner. For some western states and U.S. sectors, the South Korean market is even more important. South Korea is far more dependent economically on the United States than the United States is on South Korea. In 2010, the United States was South Korea's third-largest trading partner, second-largest export market, and the third-largest source of imports. It was among South Korea's largest suppliers of foreign direct investment (FDI).

As both economies have become more integrated with the world economy, economic interdependence has become more complex and attenuated, particularly as the United States' economic importance to South Korea has declined relative to other major powers. In 2003, China for the first time displaced the United States from its perennial place as South Korea's number one trading partner. In the mid-2000s, Japan and then the 27-member European Union also overtook the United States.

The KORUS FTA[41]

The Bush and Roh Administrations initiated the proposed KORUS FTA negotiations in 2006 and signed an agreement in June 2007. The text of the proposed free trade agreement covers a wide range of trade and investment issues and, therefore, could have wide economic implications for both the United States and South Korea. A congressionally mandated study by the United States International Trade Commission (USITC) concluded that investment and trade between the United States and South Korea would increase modestly as a result of the KORUS FTA. This result is in line with other similar studies. In general and in the short-to-medium term, the KORUS FTA's largest commercial effects are expected to be microeconomic in nature. The U.S. services and agriculture industries, for instance, are expected to reap significant benefits if the agreement is implemented. In contrast, U.S. textile, wearing apparel, and electronic equipment manufacturers would be expected to experience declines in employment from increased South Korean imports, though some U.S. electronics companies may see competitive benefits, as it could be less expensive for them to source components from South Korea.

Table 1. Annual U.S.-South Korea Merchandise Trade, Selected Years

(Billions of U.S. Dollars)				
Year	**U.S. Exports**	**U.S. Imports**	**Trade Balance**	**Total Trade**
1990	14.4	18.5	-4.1	32.9
1995	25.4	24.2	1.2	49.6
2000	26.3	39.8	-13.5	66.1
2005	26.2	43.2	-17.0	69.4
2008	33.1	46.7	-13.6	79.8
2009	27.0	38.7	-11.7	65.7
2010	38.0	48.9	-10.9	86.9
Major U.S. Export Items	Industrial machinery; specialized instruments; chemicals; civilian aircraft; transistors; semiconductor circuits; corn & wheat; semiconductor circuits; iron & steel scrap.			
Major U.S. Import Items	Motor vehicles & parts; cell phones; semiconductor circuits & printed circuit boards; machinery; iron & steel.			

Sources: 1990 and 1995 data from Global Trade Information Services. 2000-2010 data from U.S. International Trade Commission. The 2000-2010 U.S. export data are for U.S. domestic exports and the data for U.S. imports are for imports on a consumption basis.

While a broad swath of the U.S. business community supports the agreement, the original KORUS FTA was opposed by some groups, including some auto and steel manufacturers and labor unions. Following December 3, 2010, modifications to the FTA by the Obama and Lee administrations, several automotive interests—including Ford and the United Auto Workers—announced that the new auto provisions had convinced them to support the agreement. In South Korea, while public opinion polls generally show broad support for the KORUS FTA, the largest opposition party as well as many farmers and trade unionists have vocally and actively opposed the agreement.

Many observers have argued that, in addition to its economic implications, the KORUS FTA would have diplomatic and security implications. Indeed, in many respects, the KORUS FTA's fate may go beyond strengthening U.S.-Korea ties and have profound implications for U.S. trade policy and East Asia policy. For instance, some have suggested that a KORUS FTA would help to solidify the U.S. presence in East Asia to counterbalance the increasing influence of China. Some counter this by positing that the KORUS FTA need not be seen as a necessary, let alone sufficient, condition for enhancing the U.S.-ROK alliance. However, many South Koreans would likely see a failure to complete or a defeat of the agreement in part as a U.S. psychological rejection of *South Korea*. Additionally, many East Asian leaders would see such a move as a sign that the United States is disengaging from East Asia, where most countries are pursuing a variety of free trade agreements. South Korea has perhaps been the most aggressive in this FTA push. Since 2002, it has completed seven other agreements (including one with the European Union, awaiting ratification) and has begun negotiating seven others.

South Korea's Economic Performance

South Korea has recorded strong economic growth since the global financial crisis began in late 2008. After GDP real growth declined to 0.2% in 2009, the South Korean economy has roared back and grew by 6.2% in 2010. Initially, the crisis hit the South Korean economy hard because of its heavy reliance on international trade and its banks' heavy borrowing from abroad. The Lee government took strong countermeasures to blunt the crisis' impact, engaging in a series of fiscal stimulus actions worth about 6% of the country's 2008 GDP, by some measures the largest such package in the Organization for Economic Cooperation and Development (OECD) group of industrialized countries.

The Bank of Korea (BOK) also acted aggressively, lowering interest rates from over 5% to a record low 2% and engaging in a range of other operations, estimated by the OECD to be worth over 2.5% of GDP, designed to infuse liquidity in the Korean economy. The BOK negotiated currency swap agreements with the United States, Japan, and China.[42] The South Korean *won,* after depreciating to around 1,500 *won*/dollar—a fall of nearly one-third from early 2008 to early 2009—has gradually strengthened against the dollar, to the 1,000-1,100 *won*/dollar range. The *won*'s depreciation helped to stimulate South Korea's economic recovery by making its exports cheaper relative to many other currencies, particularly the Japanese *yen*.

Since the second half of 2010, South Korean real GDP growth has slowed to the 4%-5% level, in part due to the *won's* appreciation. Complaints have risen that only Korea's rich individuals and large conglomerates (called *chaebol*) have benefitted from the country's growth since the 2008-2009 slowdown. Many analysts predict that the 2012 elections will be fought over governance and social welfare issues. Leading figures in both parties, as well as President Lee, have proposed ways to expand South Korea's social safety net. Inflation, particularly due to rising oil prices, has also emerged as a concern.

OTHER ISSUES

Bilateral Nuclear Cooperation[43]

The United States and South Korea have cooperated in the peaceful use of nuclear energy for over fifty years.[44] The current U.S.-ROK bilateral nuclear cooperation agreement (or "123" agreement) expires in 2014.[45] The United States and South Korea began official talks in Washington on renewing the agreement in October 2010.[46] These talks continue, and a draft agreement was proposed by South Korea in the second round of talks in March 2011.

One point of potential disagreement in the renewal process is whether South Korea will press the United States to include a provision that would allow for the reprocessing of its spent fuel. The current U.S.-Korea nuclear cooperation agreement, as with other standard agreements,[47] requires U.S. permission before South Korea can reprocess U.S.-origin spent fuel, including spent fuel from South Korea's U.S.-designed reactors.[48] The issue has become a sensitive one for many South Korean officials and politicians, who see it as a matter of national sovereignty. The United States has been reluctant to grant such permission due to concerns over the impact on negotiations with North Korea and on the nonproliferation regime overall. Reprocessing of spent fuel can be used to make reactor fuel or to acquire plutonium for weapons.

For many years, the United States and South Korea have worked on joint research and development projects to address spent fuel disposition, including joint research on pyroprocessing, a type of spent fuel reprocessing. The Korean Atomic Energy Research Institute (KAERI) is conducting a laboratory-scale research program on reprocessing spent fuel with an advanced pyro-processing technique.[49] U.S.-South Korean bilateral research on pyro-processing began in 2002 under the Department of Energy's International Nuclear Energy Research Initiative (INERI). New R&D work on pyro-processing was halted by the United States in 2008, due to the proliferation sensitivity of the technology. In an attempt to find a way forward, in March 2010 the United States and South Korea began a six-month joint study on the economics, technical feasibility, and nonproliferation implications of pyro-processing.[50] This initial study resulted in the announcement in October 2010 of a 10-year, three-part joint research project that is separate from the 123 renewal negotiations.[51] It will include bilateral work on pyro-processing at the Idaho National Laboratory, development of international safeguards for this technology, economic viability studies, and other advanced nuclear research including alternatives to pyro-processing for spent fuel disposal.[52]

South Korean Nonproliferation Policy

South Korea has been a consistent and vocal supporter of strengthening the global nonproliferation regime. It is a member of the Nuclear Suppliers' Group and adheres to all nonproliferation treaties and export control regimes. An International Atomic Energy Agency Additional Protocol for South Korea entered into force as of February 2004. South Korea also participates in the G-8 Global Partnership, and U.S.-led initiatives—the Proliferation Security Initiative, the International Framework for Nuclear Energy Cooperation (formerly GNEP), and the Global Initiative to Combat Nuclear Terrorism.

South Korea will host the next Nuclear Security Summit in 2012.[53] At the 2010 Summit, South Korea announced it would host the next Plenary session for the Global Initiative to Combat Nuclear Terrorism in 2011 as part of its contribution to improving international nuclear security coordination.

South Korean Politics[54]

For most of the first four decades after the country was founded in 1948, South Korea was ruled by authoritarian governments. Ever since the mid-1980s, when widespread anti-government protests forced the country's military rulers to enact sweeping democratic reforms, democratic institutions and traditions have deepened in South Korea. In 1997, long-time dissident and opposition politician Kim Dae-jung (commonly referred to as "DJ") was elected to the presidency, the first time an opposition party had prevailed in a South Korean presidential election. In December 2002, Kim was succeeded by a member of his left-of-center party: Roh Moo-hyun, a self-educated former human rights lawyer who emerged from relative obscurity to defeat establishment candidates in both the primary and general elections. Roh campaigned on a platform of reform—reform of Korean politics, economic policymaking, and U.S.-ROK relations.

Lee's victory in the December 2007 election restored conservatives to the presidency. A striking feature of the election was how poorly the left-of-center candidates performed, after a decade in power, receiving only around 30% of the vote. Shortly after Lee's inauguration, his Grand National Party retained control of the National Assembly in national parliamentary elections.

Lee had a rocky first two years of his presidency. Until late 2009, his public approval ratings generally were in the 20%-30% range. It took over a year for him to recover from the massive anti-government protests that followed an April 2008 deal with the United States to lift South Korea's partial ban on imports of U.S. beef. The ban had been in place since 2003, when a cow in the United States was found to be infected with mad cow disease, or BSE (bovine spongiform encephalopathy). By the early to mid-spring of 2010, his ratings had risen to the 40%-50% range, a development many attribute to South Korea's strong recovery from the 2008-2009 global financial crisis.

South Korea's next National Assembly and presidential elections are scheduled for April and December 2012, respectively. By law, Lee cannot run again; South Korean presidents serve one five-year term.

A Powerful Executive Branch

Nominally, power in South Korea is shared by the president and the 299-member unicameral National Assembly. Of these, 245 members represent single-member constituencies. The remaining 54 are selected on the basis of

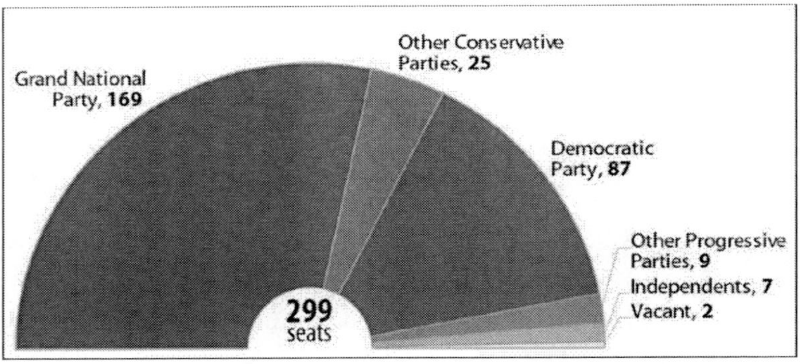

Note: Last nationwide elections held in April 2008; next elections to be held in April 2012.

Figure 3. Party Strength in South Korea's National Assembly As of June 28, 2011.

proportional voting. National Assembly members are elected to four-year terms. The president and the state bureaucracy continue to be the dominant forces in South Korean policymaking, as formal and informal limitations prevent the National Assembly from initiating major pieces of legislation.

Political Parties

Presently, there are two major political parties in South Korea: President Lee's conservative Grand National Party (GNP) and the opposition, center-left Democratic Party (DP). U.S. ties have historically been much stronger with South Korea's conservative parties. Because Korean politics tend to be hyper-partisan, this phenomenon could make U.S.-South Korea relations more difficult to manage if the progressives regain power.

The GNP's numerical strength masks significant intra-party divisions. Lee's most significant rival is GNP stalwart Park Geun-hye, the popular daughter of Korea's former military ruler Park Chung-hee, whom Lee only narrowly defeated in the GNP's presidential primary in 2007. Initially, Lee had tried to marginalize Park's influence, an effort he later abandoned when the GNP absorbed some of Park's supporters who had formed a new party. This move, however, has failed to resolve the tensions between the two camps. There is little cooperation between the GNP and the Democratic Party, so keeping the GNP unified on controversial issues is critical to Lee's ability to govern.

After the 2007 election, the Democratic Party were even more divided than the GNP. The Democrats' lack of unity, their minority status in the National Assembly, and the absence of national elections until 2012 have deprived them of most tools of power and influence within the South Korean polity. In a sign that the progressive camp may be regrouping, however, the DP scored significant victories in important local elections in June 2010. DP members and their supporters often are more critical of U.S. policies and are much more likely to support engagement policies toward North Korea than their conservative counterparts.

SELECTED CRS REPORTS ON THE KOREAS

South Korea

CRS Report RL34330, *The Proposed U.S.-South Korea Free Trade Agreement (KORUS FTA): Provisions and Implications*, coordinated by William H. Cooper

CRS Report RL34093, *The Kaesong North-South Korean Industrial Complex*, by Mark E. Manyin and Dick K. Nanto

CRS Report RL34528, *U.S.-South Korea Beef Dispute: Issues and Status*, by Remy Jurenas and Mark E. Manyin

CRS Report R4 1032, *U.S. and South Korean Cooperation in the World Nuclear Energy Market: Major Policy Considerations*, by Mark Holt

North Korea

CRS Report R41259, *North Korea: U.S. Relations, Nuclear Diplomacy, and Internal Situation*, by Emma Chanlett-Avery

CRS Report R40095, *Foreign Assistance to North Korea*, by Mark E. Manyin and Mary Beth Nikitin

CRS Report RL34256, North Korea's Nuclear Weapons: Technical Issues, by Mary Beth Nikitin

CRS Report R41438, *North Korea: Legislative Basis for U.S. Economic Sanctions*, by Dianne E. Rennack

CRS Report R41843, *Imports from North Korea: Existing Rules, Implications of the KORUS FTA, and the Kaesong Industrial Complex*, coordinated by Mark E. Manyin

CRS Report RL30613, *North Korea: Back on the Terrorism List?*, by Mark E. Manyin

CRS Report RL3 2493, *North Korea: Economic Leverage and Policy Analysis*, by Dick K. Nanto and Emma Chanlett-Avery

CRS Report RS22973, *Congress and U.S. Policy on North Korean Human Rights and Refugees: Recent Legislation and Implementation*, by Emma Chanlett-Avery

CRS Report R41043, *China-North Korea Relations*, by Dick K. Nanto and Mark E. Manyin

CRS Report RS2 1473, *North Korean Ballistic Missile Threat to the United States*, by Steven A. Hildreth

CRS Report R41749, *Non-Governmental Organizations Activities in North Korea*, by Mi Ae Taylor and Mark E. Manyin

End Notes

1 For more on the food aid debate, see CRS Report R40095, *Foreign Assistance to North Korea*, by Mark E. Manyin and Mary Beth Nikitin

2 The Blue House, Speech by President Lee Myung-bak, "The Building of an Advanced Nation will be Possible Only When We Sacrifice Ourselves for Others Rather Than Simply Pursuing Our Own Interest," December 27, 2010.

3 "U.S., Seoul Secure Plans for Potential Counterattack," Wall Street Journal. July 7, 2011.

4 Report found at http://www.gao.gov/products/GAO

5 Bruce Klingner, "Proposed Re-Realignment for Northeast Asia Ignores Strategic Realities," *Heritage Foundation WebMemo #3262*, May 18, 2011.

6 Lee is in year four of his five year term. By law, South Korean presidents cannot run for re-election.

7 In-Soo Nam, "Get Ready For The Olympic Spendathon," The Wall Street Journal, Korea Real Time blog, July 7, 2011, 5:38 PM KST.

8 International Olympic Committee Press Release, "IOC Elects PyeongChang as the Host City of 2018 Olympic Winter Games," July 6, 2011.

9 For an estimate of the number of ethnic Koreans in the United States, see U.S. Census Bureau, "The Asian Population: 2000," Census Brief C2KBR/01-16, February 2002, Table 4.

10 December 2009 interview.

11 The cause of the *Cheonan 's* sinking has become highly controversial in South Korea. While most conservatives believe that North Korea was responsible for explosion, many who lean to the left have criticized the investigation team as biased or argue that its methodology was flawed. Alternative theories for the sinking have been swirling on the Korean blogosphere. Additionally, polls indicate many if not most Koreans believe the Lee government attempted to exploit the incident during local elections held across the nation in early June. Though Lee's conservative Grand National Party suffered notable losses, polls indicate that local issues, rather than North Korea policy, were more significant factors determining voting behavior.

12 For more information, see CRS Report R41438, *North Korea: Legislative Basis for U.S. Economic Sanctions*, by Dianne E. Rennack.

[13] For more on North Korea's suspected nuclear capabilities and the diplomacy surrounding them, see CRS Report RL34256, *North Korea's Nuclear Weapons: Technical Issues*, by Mary Beth Nikitin, and CRS Report R41259, *North Korea: U.S. Relations, Nuclear Diplomacy, and Internal Situation*, by Emma Chanlett-Avery.

[14] Siegfried S. Hecker, "A Return Trip to North Korea's Yongbyon Nuclear Complex," Center for International Security and Cooperation, Stanford University, November 20, 2010.

[15] Stratfor.com, "Satellite Imagery: Tactical Details of the Korean Artillery Exchange," November 30, 2010.

[16] "DPRK KPA Supreme Command's Communique on Artillery Gunfire Along Inter-Korean Border," Pyongyang Korean Central Broadcasting Station in Korean, November 23, 2010, translated by Open Source Center KPP20101123106004; "DPRK Commentary Says 23 Nov Clash Due to US, Civilian Casualties 'Very Regrettable'," Korean Central News Agency, November 27, 2010.

[17] "'Full Text' of ROK President Lee's 29 November 'Address to the Nation,'" *Yonhap*, November 29, 2010. Lee said that for decades, South Korea had "tolerated provocations by the North time and again.... South Korea nonetheless endured these continual provocations because we entertained a slight hope that the North would change course someday.... At long last, we came to a realization that ... that prolonged endurance and tolerance will spawn nothing but more serious provocations. If the North commits any additional provocations against the South, we will make sure that it pays a dear price without fail."

[18] See, for instance, State Department Press Release, "Trilateral Statement Japan, Republic of Korea, and the United States," December 6, 2010.

[19] Some figures quantify the downturn in relations from 2007 to 2008: official bilateral dialogues were down from 55 in 2007 to 6 in 2008; South Korea's governmental humanitarian assistance declined from 3.5 million *won* ($215 million) to 0.4 million *won* ($25 million); and government-run reunions of family members fell from over 3,600 to zero. After years of double-digit growth, inter-Korean trade registered a mere 1.2% increase from 2007 to 2008. Figures are from Ministry of Unification, "Inter-Korean Relations in 2008," February 2009. North-South Korean trade was just over $1.8 billion in 2008.

[20] Four actions by North Korea have had a particularly dramatic impact on South Korea's policy toward the North: the refusal to allow an independent South Korean investigation into the July 2008 fatal shooting of a South Korean tourist by a North Korean soldier at the Mt. Kumgang resort in North Korea, a nuclear test in May 2009, periodically placing greater restrictions on the inter-Korean industrial complex at Kaesong, and the sinking of the *Cheonan*.

[21] For more, see CRS Report RL34093, *The Kaesong North-South Korean Industrial Complex*, by Mark E. Manyin and Dick K. Nanto.

[22] Christian Oliver, "Seoul Plans $40bn Aid Fund for N Korea," *Financial Times*, July 20, 2009. North Korea's 2009 per capita income was $1,900, according to the CIA *World Factbook*.

[23] From 1999-2007, trilateral summits were only held on the sidelines of the Association of Southeast Asian Nations' "Plus Three" summit (which included the 10 ASEAN countries plus China, Japan, and South Korea).

[24] Many Koreans believe that the United States was complicit in this history, by reportedly informally agreeing in a 1905 meeting between U.S. Secretary of War William Taft and Japanese Prime Minister Taro Katsura that the United States would recognize Japan's sphere of influence over Korea in return for Japan doing the same for the United States in the Philippines.

[25] Much of South Korea's exports to China are intermediate goods that ultimately are used in products exported to the United States and Europe.

[26] "U.S. Army in South Korea Begins Transformation of Forces," *Stars and Stripes*. August 25, 2010.

[27] "South Korea Approves FY10 Defence Budget," *Jane's Defence Industry*. January 4, 2010.

[28] "Defense Ministry Seeks 31.2 Trillion Won Budget for 2011," *Yonhap English News*, September 28, 2010, and "Parliamentary Committee Approves Defense Budget Increase," *Yonhap English News*, November 30, 2010.

[29] "Analysis of ROK Defense Budget for 2011," *ROK Angle* Issue 48, Korea Institute for Defense Analyses, April 19, 2011.

[30] "US-South Korea: a New Security Relationship," *Jane's Intelligence Weekly*, January 18, 2010.

[31] "Senate Armed Services Committee Holds Hearing on Security Situation on the Korean Peninsula," *CQ Congressional Transcripts*. September 16, 2010.

[32] "Sharp: Korea Plan Synchronizes Capabilities," PACOM Headlines, *American Forces Press Service*. September 21, 2010.

[33] Joint United States Military Affairs Group – Korea Mission Brief. August 18, 2010.

[34] "South Korea to Buy More U.S. Weapons to Counter North," *Reuters*. September 21, 2010.

[35] "South Korea Pulls Back from Original Defense Spending Plan Amid Economic Woes," *Yonhap News*. September 27, 2009.

[36] "Seoul Deploys Precision-guided Missiles Targeting Pyongyang," *Korea Herald*. June 28, 2011.

[37] "Next-Generation MLRS Named 'Cheonmu," *KBS*. June 28, 2011.

[38] "South Korea Defense Budget," *Jane's Defence Budgets*. December 14, 2009.

[39] "Korea's T-50 Spreads Its Wings," *Defense Industry Insider*. September 13, 2010.

[40] In 2007, South Korean President Roh Moo-hyun withdrew South Korea's initial deployment of 200 non-combat military personnel from Afghanistan after the Taliban kidnapped South Korean missionaries. The South Korean government reportedly paid a sizeable ransom to the Taliban to secure the release of kidnapped South Korean Christian missionaries, reported by one Taliban official to be $20 million.

[41] For more information, please see CRS Report RL34330, *The Proposed U.S.-South Korea Free Trade Agreement (KORUS FTA): Provisions and Implications*, coordinated by William H. Cooper.

42 The October 2008 swap agreement with the U.S. Federal Reserve gave Bank of Korea access to up to USD 30 billion in US dollar funds in exchange for *won*.

[43] Written by Mary Beth Nikitin, Specialist in Nonproliferation.

[44] The original agreement was concluded in 1956, and amendments were made in 1958, 1965, 1972 and 1974. See also CRS Report R41032, *U.S. and South Korean Cooperation in the World Nuclear Energy Market: Major Policy Considerations*, by Mark Holt.

[45] Full text at http://nnsa.energy.com

[46] "Discussions on the New U.S.-R.O.K. Civil Nuclear Cooperation Agreement State Department Press Release, October 26, 2010.

[47] CRS Report RS22937, *Nuclear Cooperation with Other Countries: A Primer*, by Paul K. Kerr and Mary Beth Nikitin.

[48] Under the 1978 Nuclear Nonproliferation Act, consent rights apply to material originating in the U.S. or material that has been fabricated into fuel or irradiated in a reactor with U.S. technology. The majority of South Korea's spent fuel would need U.S. consent before it could be reprocessed.

[49] Pyro-processing technology would partially separate plutonium and uranium from spent fuel.

[50] http://www.koreaherald.co.kr/NEWKHSITE/data/html_dir/2010/03/17/201003170029.asp.

[51] "Discussions on Korea-U.S. Joint Research on Fuel Cycle," Press Release, Ministry of Education, Science and Technology, Republic of Korea, April 18, 2011.

[52] "S. Korea, U.S. Agree to Start Joint Study on Nuclear Fuel Reprocessing," *Yonhap*, April 17, 2011.

[53] See also, CRS Report R41 169, *Securing Nuclear Materials: The 2010 Summit and Issues for Congress*, by Mary Beth Nikitin.

[54] For more, see CRS Report R40851, *South Korea: Its Domestic Politics and Foreign Policy Outlook*, by Mark E. Manyin and Weston Konishi.

In: South Korea
Editors: A. L. Hines and D. O. Mullins
ISBN: 978-1-61942-377-0

Chapter 4

THE KAESONG NORTH-SOUTH KOREAN INDUSTRIAL COMPLEX[1]

Mark E. Manyin and Dick K. Nanto

SUMMARY

This purpose of this report is to provide an overview of the role, purposes, and results of the Kaesong Industrial Complex (KIC) and examine U.S. interests, policy issues, options, and legislation. The KIC is a six-year-old industrial park located in the Democratic People's Republic of Korea (DPRK or North Korea) just across the demilitarized zone from South Korea. As of the end of 2010, over 120 medium-sized South Korean companies were employing over 47,000 North Korean workers to manufacture products in Kaesong. The facility, which in 2010 produced $323 million in output, has the land and infrastructure to house two to three times as many firms and workers. Products vary widely, and include clothing and textiles (71 firms), kitchen utensils (4 firms), auto parts (4 firms), semiconductor parts (2 firms), and toner cartridges (1 firm).

Despite a rise in tensions between North and South Korea since early 2008, the complex has continued to operate and expand. The KIC was not shut down in 2010 despite two violent incidents between the two Koreas that year: the March sinking of a South Korean naval vessel, the *Cheonan*, which was

[1] This is an edited, reformatted and augmented version of the Congressional Research Service report, dated April 2011.

found to be caused by a North Korean torpedo, and North Korea's artillery attack on a South Korean island in November. Indeed, the complex has become virtually the last vestige of inter-Korean cooperation. After the *Cheonan* sinking, South Korea announced it would cut off all inter-Korean economic relations except the Kaesong complex. It also has reduced the number of South Korean workers—primarily government officials and business managers—at the complex because of worries about them being taken hostage by North Korea.

The KIC represents a dilemma for U.S. and South Korean policymakers. On the one hand, the project provides an ongoing revenue stream to the Kim Jong-il regime in Pyongyang, by virtue of the share the government takes from the salaries paid to North Korean workers. South Korean and U.S. officials estimate this revenue stream to be around $20 million per year. On the other hand, the KIC arguably helps maintain stability on the Peninsula and provides a possible beachhead for market reforms in the DPRK that could eventually spill over to areas outside the park and expose tens of thousands of North Koreans to outside influences, market-oriented businesses, and incentives.

The United States has limited direct involvement in the KIC, which the United States has officially supported since its conception. At present, no U.S. companies have invested in the Kaesong complex, though a number of South Korean officials have expressed a desire to attract U.S. investment. U.S. government approval is needed for South Korean firms to ship to the KIC certain U.S.-made equipment currently under U.S. export controls. The Korea-U.S. Free Trade Agreement (KORUS FTA), which has yet to be submitted to Congress for approval, provides for a Committee on Outward Processing Zones (OPZ) to be formed and to consider whether zones such as the KIC will receive preferential treatment under the FTA. The KORUS FTA says that the executive branch will seek "legislative approval" for any changes to the agreement. The Obama Administration says this would take the form of a law to extend any KORUS tariff benefits to products made in Kaesong or any OPZ.

Another issue raised by the KIC is whether components made in the complex can enter the United States if they are incorporated into products that are manufactured in South Korea and that qualify as originating in South Korea. This possibility is likely to be determined mainly by the KIC's evolution; the more that is produced in the complex, the more products are likely to enter South Korea's supply chain.

Table 1. Key Statistics for the Kaesong Industrial Complex

	End 2005	End 2006	End 2007	End 2008	End 2009	End 2010
No. of South Korean Manufacturing Firms	11	15	65	93	118	121
					(Jan. 2010)	
Approx. No. of North Korean Workers	6,000	11,000	23,000	39,000	42,000	47,000
Approx. No. of South Korean Workers	n.a.	700	800	1,500	960	Around 500
Annual Production Value	$15 mil.	$74 mil.	$185 mil.	$250 mil.	$256 mil	$323 mil
Exports to 3rd Countries (i.e., not South Korea)	–	$20 mil.	$40 mil	$36 mil	$29 mil	$37 mil

Sources: South Korean Ministry of Unification documents.

DEVELOPMENTS FROM MARCH 2010-JUNE 2010

The Kaesong Industrial Complex (KIC) is an industrial park located in the Democratic People's Republic of Korea (DPRK or North Korea) just across the demilitarized zone from South Korea. As of the end of December 2010, approximately 120 medium-sized South Korean companies were using North Korean labor to manufacture products there, employing over 47,000 workers. (See Table 1.) Currently, the park has much of the infrastructure (e.g., South Korean-built water, sewage treatment, and electrical facilities) to enable the completion of the complex's first phase, an 800-acre site that would contain roughly 300 foreign manufacturers employing around 100,000 North Korean workers. If the master plan of Hyundai Asan, the co-developer of the project, is followed the KIC eventually will be over 6,000 acres (nearly half the size of Manhattan Island) and include high-technology zones, shopping districts, residential areas, and facilities for tourism and recreation. At present, over 100 companies that have signed lease agreements to open factories have not done so. The complex was planned, developed, and financed largely by South Korea, and it has become a symbol of engagement between the North and the South. In 2010, about $1.4 billion, or 76%, of the $1.9 billion in total trade between the two Koreas was attributable to the KIC.[1]

The purpose of this report is to provide an overview of the role, purposes, and results of the KIC and examine U.S. interests, policy issues, options, and legislation.

The KIC Survives Inter-Korean Tensions in 2010

Twice in 2010, the KIC 's future was thrown into doubt by a marked deterioration in inter-Korean relations. First, on March 26, 2010, a South Korean naval vessel, the *Cheonan*, sank in waters disputed by the two Koreas. Nearly 50 South Korean sailors died in the incident. A multinational investigation team led by South Korea determined that the ship was sunk by a North Korean submarine.[2] South Korea, backed by the United States and Japan, has said it will take the case before the United Nations Security Council. On May 24, 2010, South Korean President Lee Myung-bak also announced that North Korean ships would no longer be permitted to pass through shipping lanes under South Korean control, and that North-South trade, visits, and exchanges generally would be suspended. Exceptions were made for humanitarian aid to infants and children, and for the KIC. Propaganda radio and loudspeaker broadcasts into North Korea would also be resumed.[3] South Korean Minister of Unification Hyun In-taek announced that new investments in the complex would be stopped and that the number of South Korean personnel at the complex—which had often approached 1,000 people in mid-week—would be reduced by as much as 50%.[4]

North Korea's Committee for the Peaceful Reunification of the Fatherland, the government organ responsible for inter-Korean relations, responded by labeling the actions by the "puppet" South Korean government as "a declaration of war against us" and announcing that it would abrogate all North-South non-aggression agreements, terminate contact with Lee's government, and "completely halt" all North-South cooperation projects, among other steps.[5] However, the Kaesong complex was not shut down, although North Korea threatened to take this step if South Korean loudspeaker broadcasts resumed. (It also threatened to shoot at the loudspeakers.) Instead, several South Korean government workers at the KIC were expelled. South Korea did not restart its broadcasts.

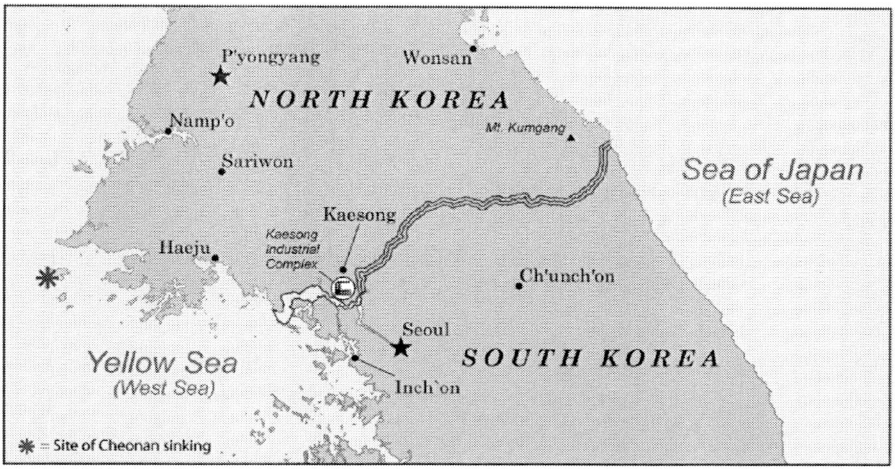

Source: Prepared by CRS based on ESRI Data and Maps 9.3.1; IHS World Data.

Figure 1. The Kaesong Industrial Complex and the North-South Korean Border.

Second, on November 23, North Korean artillery units fired over 150 shells onto and around Yeonpyeong Island, across the North-South disputed western sea border. North Korea claimed that the South Korean military had fired first, during routine U.S.-ROK exercises in the area. According to one report, about half the North Korean shells hit the island. The barrage killed four South Koreans (two marines and two civilians), wounded dozens, and destroyed or damaged scores of homes and other buildings.[6] It was North Korea's first direct artillery attack on ROK territory since the 1950-1953 Korean War. South Korea responded by shooting 80 shells at North Korea. An official North Korean media outlet later said that the South Korean civilian deaths were "regrettable."[7]

The attacks prompted South Korea and the United States to hold large-scale naval exercises in the Yellow Sea area with the USS *George Washington* aircraft carrier strike group and led to closer U.S.-South Korea-Japan collaboration on security matters. In a nationally televised speech, Lee announced that South Korea would no longer hold back on retaliating for North Korean provocations. The South Korean defense minister stated that if attacked in the future, South Korea would consider using its air force to strike back in North Korean territory.[8]

Despite these tensions, it appeared that both Koreas were reluctant to allow the complex to be closed, or at least to be blamed for its closure. Aside from the park's symbolic importance, both sides would incur financial losses if it ceased operating. The KIC provides the North Korean government with a constant revenue stream of around $2 million a month, by virtue of the share the government takes from the salaries paid to North Korean workers. The prospect of triggering social unrest due to depriving families in the Kaesong area, with a population of around 200,000, of high-paying jobs may also be a factor for the North Korean regime of Kim Jong-il, who is trying to pave the way for his son, Kim Jong-un, to succeed him.

As for South Korea, a closure could make the central government liable for hundreds of millions of dollars in insurance payments to the South Korean companies that use the park. Although there have been conflicting reports about whether South Korean manufacturers in the park are profitable, it is possible that a number of them would suffer significant financial hardship if the KIC were closed.

The up and down treatment of the Kaesong complex in 2010 fits the patterns that have existed for the past three years.

The KIC and Inter-Korean Relations

The KIC is virtually the last vestige of the range of inter-Korean cooperation projects initiated during the period of détente between South Korea and North Korea from 2000-2008. Relations began deteriorating after new developments in both Koreas. In December 2007, a new, conservative South Korean president, Lee Myung-bak, was elected. Lee's administration cancelled a range of large-scale infrastructure inter-Korean projects that his predecessor had promised South Korea would finance, instituted a more "reciprocity-based" policy toward North Korea, and was openly critical of human rights conditions in North Korea. Lee has linked progress on a number of items in inter-Korean relations to North Korea's agreement to denuclearize.

Lee's government has been ambivalent about KIC. On one hand, the complex has been physically expanding since Lee took office. As shown in Table 1, the number of South Korean manufacturers operating in the complex has nearly doubled since his inauguration in early 2008.[9] Under Lee, a number of steps have been taken to support the KIC, including providing special tax breaks to small and medium-sized enterprises that outsource their manufacturing to KIC companies; allowing KIC companies to resell their lots inside the complex; reducing health care premiums by 50% for South Korean workers in the complex; and issuing new loans and trade insurance to KIC companies.[10]

On the other hand, the Lee administration has halted plans for a major expansion of the complex. Of the 57 South Korean firms that have opened factories in Kaesong since Lee took office, only 7 received approval from his government. In October 2007, with the complex outgrowing the greater Kaesong area's ability to provide workers, Lee's predecessor, Roh Moo-hyun (2003- 2008), promised North Korea that Seoul would build dormitories to house tens of thousands of new North Korean workers. Lee cancelled these plans. It is unclear to what extent his government will link construction of the dorms to North Korea's behavior in nuclear talks and/or to some sort of apology for the *Cheonan* sinking and the Yeonpyeong Island attack. Alternatively, the Lee government may decide to link the dorms to developments within the park. For instance, many South Koreans want more provisions for the safety of South Korean workers at the complex and to allow greater communication services (such as cell phones, which currently are prohibited at the complex).

In North Korea, Kim Jong-il's reported stroke in the summer of 2008 coincided with a more bellicose and provocative stance, including the testing of a nuclear device in May 2009. For roughly a nine-month period from November 2008 through August 2009, the North Korean military appeared to be dictating policy decisions with regard to the KIC. During this time, North Korean authorities imposed a number of restrictions on the KIC, including closing down the border for several days in March 2009, effectively trapping hundreds of South Korean workers at the complex. The restrictions are blamed for the decline in the complex's aggregate production in 2009. The apparent reassertion of civilian control in the late summer of 2009—the time period when Kim Jong-il is commonly thought to have reasserted his authority—brought a relaxation of most of the restrictions. North Korea also stepped back from demands it had made that investors dramatically increase wages and payments.

Implications for U.S. Interests

The KIC represents a policy dilemma. On the one hand, as mentioned above, the project provides an ongoing revenue stream to the Kim Jong-il regime in Pyongyang. On the other hand, the KIC provides a possible beachhead for market reforms in the DPRK that could eventually spill over to areas outside the park and expose tens of thousands of North Koreans to outside influences and incentives. Expanding the park would exacerbate the dilemma: The regime would reap additional funds, but bringing in workers from areas north of Kaesong could also enhance the park's potential to serve as a "Trojan horse" in the medium-to-long term. The original plans for the KIC envisioned the complex eventually housing hundreds of foreign (i.e., non-North Korean) manufacturers, employing hundreds of thousands of North Korean workers.

The United States has limited direct involvement in the KIC, which the United States has officially supported since its conception. At present, no U.S. companies have invested in the Kaesong complex, though a number of South Korean officials have expressed a desire to attract U.S. investment. U.S. government approval is needed for South Korean firms to ship to the KIC certain U.S.-made equipment currently under U.S. export controls. The Korea-U.S. Free Trade Agreement (KORUS FTA), which has yet to be submitted to Congress for approval, provides for a Committee on Outward Processing Zones (OPZ) to be formed and to consider whether zones such as the KIC will receive preferential treatment under the FTA (see "Kaesong and the Proposed Korea-U.S. Free Trade Agreement" below). The EU-Korea FTA, which was signed in 2009, contains a similar provision.

THE DEVELOPMENT OF THE KAESONG INDUSTRIAL COMPLEX

The KIC resulted from an initiative led by the Hyundai Group beginning in 1998 that coincided with the Republic of Korea's (ROK) "sunshine policy" that attempted to improve relations between South Korea and the DPRK. The KIC is located about 106 miles southeast of Pyongyang and 43 miles north of Seoul just across the demilitarized zone (DMZ) in the DPRK. The purposes of the KIC as stated by South Korea have been to develop an industrial park in which South Korean businesses could manufacture products using North Korean labor, provide an opening for North Korea to liberalize and reform its economy, and ease tensions across the DMZ. Although begun primarily as a private sector venture, both governments are heavily involved in the project. Groundbreaking occurred in June 2003 and again in April 2004. Hyundai Asan and the Korea Land Corporation (both from South Korea) have been developing and managing the complex.

South Korean companies operating in Kaesong receive certain incentives from the ROK government and have certain rights as determined by negotiated agreements with the DPRK. The KIC is a duty-free zone, with no restrictions on the use of foreign currency or credit cards and no visa required for entry or exit. Property and inheritance rights are ensured. South Korean law breakers in Kaesong are not to go on trial in the North.[11] The corporate tax rate is 10% to 14% with an exemption for the first five years after generating profits and a 50% reduction for the ensuing three years. The South Korean government (through its Inter-Korea Cooperation Fund) offered companies that established their operations in the KIC (in the pilot project and first phase) loans with low interest rates equal to those applied to public works projects. These loans totaled about $40 million as of the end of 2005.[12] Out of the first 26 firms to either begin operations or contemplate beginning operations in the near term, 25 of them applied for loans from the Inter- Korea Cooperation Fund.[13] South Korea also provides political risk insurance that will cover financial losses up to 90% of a company's investment in the KIC up to 5 billion South Korean won ($5.4 million). Under a South Korean law passed in April 2007, South Korean small and medium-sized firms operating in the KIC are eligible for state subsidies and other benefits equal to their counterparts at home. [14]

Table 2 shows the first three phases of the master plan for the project. The first phase encompasses 800 acres with as many as 300 South Korean firms operating in the complex. At the end of phase 3, the plan calls for as much as 4,800 acres in the industrial zone with as many as 1,500 firms employing 350,000 North Korean workers and producing $16 billion worth of products per year. It also includes 2,200 acres in a supporting zone with residential facilities (dorms), commercial establishments (hotels, restaurants, offices, conference rooms), and tourist facilities (golf course, peace park, theme park). The Master Plan also includes an Expansion Zone of 1,600 acres for industrial use and 4,000 acres for support. This would be used after phase 3 and would accommodate an additional 500 companies, 150,000 employees, and estimated production of $4 billion per year. Counting the expansion zone, the grand totals for the Master Plan would be 6,400 acres for the Industrial Zone (10 square miles), 6,200 acres for the Supporting Zone, 2,000 companies, 500,000 workers, and $20 billion per year in products. The industrial and supporting zones together cover an area roughly one-fifth the size of Washington, DC.

Table 2. Hyundai's Original Concept of the First Three Phases of the Master Plan for the Kaesong Industrial Complex

Year	Phase 1 (includes pilot) 2002-2007	Phase 2 2006-2009	Phase 3 2008-2012
Total Land at Completion of Stage	800 acres in Industrial Zone. Kaesong City as a Supporting Zone	2,000 acres in Industrial Zone 800 acres in Supporting Zone	4,800 acres in Industrial Zone 1,600 acres in Supporting Zone
Total ROK Firms at Completion of Stage	300	800	1,500
Total DPRK Workers at Completion of Stage	100,000	200,000	350,000

Source: ROK, Ministry of Unification.

The KIC aims to attract South Korean companies, particularly small and medium-sized enterprises, seeking lower labor and other costs for their manufactured products as an alternative to establishing subsidiaries in China or other low-wage markets. As indicated in Table 1, by the end of 2010, about 120 companies had begun operations in Kaesong and were employing over 47,000 North Korean workers.

Of the $374 million initial cost for the first stage, $223 million was to be provided by the South Korean government. Much of the supporting infrastructure has been built, including a job training center, a water supply plant (which sends about one-quarter of its 60,000 tons/day capacity to Kaesong City), a wastewater treatment plant, and an electricity substation. In December 2006, the Korea Electric Power Corporation connected North Korea and South Korea by a 100,000 kilowatt power-transmission line and in June 2007 began transmission of high-voltage electricity for use by the companies in the KIC. In December 2007, the two Koreas announced what was to be daily train service across the demilitarized zone along a recently reconnected rail line between the two Koreas. Regular train service, however, has not begun. The plan is for the trains to connect the KIC to South Korea in the south and to China in the north. Currently, the trains terminate south of Kaesong, in Bongdong, which does not have loading facilities.[15] Meanwhile, Kaesong is connected to South Korea by a road that has thousands of vehicles per day passing through the checkpoints.

Table 3. Production by Category in the Kaesong Industrial Complex (US $1,000)

	Textiles and Clothing	Chemical Products	Metals and Machinery	Electric and Electronic Products	Other	Total
2005	6,780	1,768	5,250	1,108	-	14,906
2006	27,793	10,900	20,853	14,191	-	73,737
2007	85,543	18,262	41,947	39,027	-	184,779
2008	132,179	21,785	49,250	47,162	1,046	251,422
2009	152,050	26,179	37,312	37,584	3,350	256,475
2010	179,235	32,092	48,637	59,147	4,212	323,323
	71 firms	9 firms	23 firms	13 firms	5 firms	121 firms

Source: ROK, Ministry of Unification documents.

The 15 companies operating in the Pilot Industrial Complex in Kaesong in 2006 and their products included Sonoko Cuisine Ware (kitchenware), SJ Tech (semiconductor component containers), Shinwon (apparel), Samduk Trading (footwear), Bucheon Industrial (wire harness), Taesung Industrial (cosmetics containers), Daewha Fuel Pump (automobile parts), Munchang Co. (apparel), Romanson (watches, jewelry), Hosan Ace (fan coils), Magic Micro (lamp assemblies for LCD monitors), JY Solutec (automobile components and molds), TS Precision Machinery (semiconductor mold components), Yongin Electronics (transformers, coils), and JCCOM (communication components).[16]

As shown in Table 3, in 2010, the KIC-produced goods totaled $323.3 million, about a 25% increase from 2009. As of the end of December 2010, a little over half of the cumulative production total had been in textiles and clothing, around 20% had been in electronics products as well as in metals/machinery, and about 10% had been in chemical products. The share of textile and clothing production has increased over time, from 46% in 2007 to 53% in 2009.[17] Examples of the variety of products made in Kaesong include socks, pajamas, shoes, auto parts (four firms), semiconductor parts (two firms), toner cartridges (one firm), fish nets, and motorcycle helmets.

Currently, all products made in the KIC are shipped to South Korea for sale there or for export after clearing customs in the ROK. The primary export destinations in 2010 were Australia, the European Union, Russia, and China. Other than labor, land, and site construction materials, there now is no local procurement of inputs into the manufacturing processes in the KIC nor are products manufactured in the KIC sold in North Korean markets. Most companies there use labor-intensive manufacturing processes with raw materials and intermediate goods from South Korea shipped to Kaesong for final assembly. As the KIC is expanded, however, companies could procure some of their manufacturing inputs locally.[18]

It is not yet clear whether South Korean companies operating in the KIC are doing so primarily for political purposes or whether their operations in the complex are economically viable. Also, it is not clear whether companies in the complex would be economically viable without South Korean government support in providing infrastructure and loans with below-market interest rates. The KIC does provide small and medium-sized businesses access to labor costs lower than those in China or Vietnam, a workforce that speaks the same language, and proximity to large markets in South Korea. Some companies appear to be using production in Kaesong to replace that in China, South Korea, or elsewhere, but others may be using government-subsidized loans and political risk insurance to invest in politically popular projects. The long list of companies that have applied to enter the KIC, however, indicates that investments there likely are seen as profitable for most businesses. It also should be noted that an estimated 40% of the small and medium-sized South Korean companies that established operations in China have not been successful there. Many have withdrawn from that market. The KIC is viewed as essential for survival by some of these companies.[19]

The experience of some of the early investors in Kaesong may be indicative of the economic viability of the project. ShinWon (clothing) established operations in the KIC to take advantage of the dexterity and lower cost of North Korean workers, favorable logistics, and to avoid nontariff barriers in China and Southeast Asia. By manufacturing about 16% of five of its clothing lines there, it expects to accrue considerable savings in production costs. It considers its Kaesong factory to be optimal when compared with those it has in China, Indonesia, Vietnam, and Guatemala.[20]

Samduk Trading Company produces high-quality shoes in the KIC. Start-up costs were high because of the need to train workers. It took eight months for some production lines to reach 60% of the productivity level of South Korean companies. The Romanson company (watches) finds the KIC superior to production in China because of the common language and low labor costs. It reportedly plans to move 75% of its watch production to the KIC. The Moonchang company (uniforms, seat covers, leisure clothes) faced a rough start in dealing with its North Korean workers but feels it is now on the right track. The Woori Bank is in a difficult situation because of the limited customer base and low demand for personal or business loans. Its main business is currency exchange. It provides zero interest rates on deposits because there are no means to make profits by investing deposits elsewhere in North Korea.[21]

Issues Related to the Kaesong Industrial Complex

The KIC has raised several issues with U.S. policy makers. These include labor conditions, financial benefits for Pyongyang, the KIC in the KORUS FTA, and the control of U.S. exports to Kaesong.

Labor Issues

A question with respect to the KIC has been the conditions for North Korean workers there and whether they are being exploited.[22] In January 2007, Jay Lefkowitz, President Bush's special envoy for human rights in North Korea, wrote that one of the concerns he had with the Kaesong Industrial Complex is that authorities take a portion (as much as 45%) of the wages paid by the South Korean companies. He noted that verified details are elusive, and neither the DPRK nor South Korean government, nor any company, has been able to state definitively how much of his or her wage a Kaesong worker is allowed to keep.[23]

According to South Korean officials, average wages and working conditions at Kaesong are far better than those in the rest of North Korea.[24] The monthly minimum wage is $60.78, or between $2 and $3 per day. On top of the minimum wage, companies pay the North Korean authorities a 15% social insurance fee providing for unemployment and occupational hazards. Increases in the minimum wage are capped at 5% per year. The minimum wage has risen from $50 per month when the park opened in 2004. General workers receive the base rate, while team leaders and heads of companies receive more. Workers also receive overtime pay.[25] For extended working hours, the overtime premium is 50% of the hourly wage rate. For public holidays and nighttime work (10 p.m. to 6 a.m.), the overtime premium is 100% of the hourly wage rate. In some cases, North Korean workers have asked for additional night shift or weekend work in order to qualify for additional pay.[26] Companies also may pay cash rewards as a special incentive. Many employees received $20-$30 per month in overtime pay. Thus, adding the minimum wage, the 15% social insurance fee, and the overtime payments, it appears that KIC manufacturers pay around $100 per month for each employee.

KIC employees receive 14 days per year in vacation time. At first, North Korean workers were reluctant to ask for leave time, but now they do.[27] Female employees receive 60 days paid maternity leave.[28] As of 2006, labor costs in Kaesong are approximately 8% of those in a South Korean metropolitan area.[29] South Korean labor laws extend to South Korean workers in the KIC.[30]

The wages of North Korean workers are paid in dollars (or other hard currency other than South Korean won) first to the Central Special Direct General Bureau, a North Korean government agency. Article 34 of the Labor Law of the Kaesong Industrial Complex, however, states that wages must be paid directly to employees in cash. The DPRK claims that this is not being implemented now because of the lack of foreign exchange centers in the KIC.[31] In 2007, the ROK Ministry of Unification stated that of the $57.50 minimum monthly salary at the time, $7.50 or 15% of the base pay went for social insurance. The North Korean government also deducted $15, or 30%, for a socio-cultural policy fee that goes for rental of state-owned housing, education, medical services, social insurance, and social welfare and reportedly is given to the Kaesong City People's Committee. According to the ministry, the remaining $35 was paid to the workers in cash (in North Korean won) or as chits that could be exchanged for daily supplies (food and necessities).[32] At the exchange rate of 140 North Korean won per dollar at the time, the $35 translated into 4,900 won. (A kilogram of rice cost about 44 won if bought from North Korea's public distribution system but as much as 1,000 won if bought on the open market. The average family consumes about 60 kilograms of rice per month.)[33] Companies provide the workers with a way to verify their wages by having them sign a ledger or provide a pay slip when they receive their pay.

North Korean workers commute to the KIC by bus provided by the Kaesong Industrial Complex Management Council and by some 1,000 bicycles also provided for workers living closer to the complex. According to the KIC Management Council, the health condition of workers at the KIC has visibly improved as they have had access to better nutrition.[34]

The actual recruitment of workers is done by North Korea's Central Guidance Agency on Special Zone Development, a cabinet level administrative body. The South Korean hiring company, however, may reject any recruit provided or if the recruit does not demonstrate the requisite skills (e.g., sewing), hire the worker as a trainee at 70% or less of the minimum wage. Employers cannot freely punish or fire incompetent workers. They must give instructions through North Korean mid-level managers. Directly scolding employees is regarded as humiliation and prohibited.[35] The experience of many companies, however, is that labor management is a challenge during the start-up phase of a factory in the KIC. Gradually, however, North Korean workers begin to identify with the company, and a level of trust is developed between the South Korean executives and the North Korean managers and workers.[36]

Currently, North Korean workers do not have the right to change employers. This promises to keep labor costs from escalating as they have in other developing markets as foreign firms bid for skilled workers. This also provides companies in the KIC with a stable (though aging) workforce.[37] This practice, however, conflicts with what would be consistent with internationally accepted workers' rights.

Financial Benefits for Pyongyang

A key aspect of the KIC for U.S. interests is how much the North Korean government derives in hard currency from the project, including leasing fees and its share of the wages of North Korean workers. The wages are first paid in hard currency (dollars) to a North Korean government agency that deducts for certain items before paying the North Korean workers in won or in chits to be exchanged for food and necessities. South Korean and U.S. government officials estimate that the North Korean government collects around $2 million per month, primarily from social insurance taxes and a socio-cultural fee deducted from the wages received by North Korean workers (the socio-cultural fee reportedly goes to the Kaesong city, not the central government). In addition, there are land lease fees and other payments to the North Korean government. When the project was initiated, Hyundai Asan paid North Korea $12 million for a 50-year lease on the entire Kaesong site. Hyundai Asan and the Korea Land Co. also purchase sand and gravel and other raw materials from North Korea for use in site development at Kaesong, though these purchases effectively came to a halt in 2010.[38] Companies in the KIC also pay North Korea's job reference agency (recruiting agency) a commission of $17 per employee sent.[39]

Under an agreement on taxation, businesses in the KIC are subject to a 10% to 14% corporate income tax, but the tax has an exemption for five years after first generating profits and a 50% deduction for the ensuing three years. This compares favorably to corporate tax rates in South Korea (12% to 28%), China (15%), and in Vietnam (10% to 15%).[40]

In 2004, the Hyundai Research Institute estimated that North Korea could receive $9.55 billion in economic gains over the course of nine years if the KIC were to be developed fully and operated successfully. This would include $4.6 billion in foreign currency earnings with $700 million derived directly from the operation of the KIC, $2.5 billion from sales of raw materials and other industrial products, and $1.4 billion from corporate taxes.[41] Considering that in international trade in goods in 2005, North Korea exported $1.8 billion and imported $3.6 billion, the estimated total gains of $9.55 billion over nine years associated with the Kaesong Industrial Complex would be quite significant (provided it progresses according to plan).

Kaesong and the Proposed Korea-U.S. Free Trade Agreement

Negotiating History

During the negotiations on the KORUS FTA, South Korea requested that products exported from the complex be considered to have originated in South Korea in order to qualify for duty-free status under the proposed FTA. Under the South Korea-ASEAN FTA, for example, preferential tariffs are applied to 100 items manufactured in the Kaesong Industrial Complex.[42] The Korea-Singapore and Korea-European Free Trade Association (EFTA) FTA agreements also include products from the KIC.[43] Singapore accepts 88.6% of the traded products from the KIC as long as no products are directly exported from the DPRK. The Korean FTA with EFTA limits coverage to 2.9% of the total trade and only for those exports that have first been brought into the South Korean territory and which have 60% of the total materials cost as South Korean.[44] In the negotiations between South Korea and the European Union, Seoul requested products from Kaesong be covered by the proposed FTA. The final 2009 EU-South Korea FTA, however, contains a provision similar to that included in the KORUS FTA.[45] In 2006, the European Union (15 nations) imported $185.7 million worth of goods from North Korea. Switzerland imported $0.8 million and Singapore $6.6 million.

For the United States, however, from the beginning of the FTA negotiations, the U.S. position was that only products originating in South Korea would be included.[46] At a U.S. House International Relations Committee hearing on July 20, 2006, Assistant U.S. Trade Representative Karan Bhatia indicated that the proposed FTA would not cover goods made in a free-trade zone in North Korea.[47]

The KORUS FTA's Text

The text of the Korea-U.S. Free Trade Agreement (signed by representatives of each government but not yet approved by Congress) does not provide for duty-free entry into the United States for products made in the Kaesong Industrial Complex. Annex 22-B to the proposed FTA, however, provides for a Committee on Outward Processing Zones (OPZ) on the Korean Peninsula to be formed and to "identify geographic areas that may be designated outward processing zones," determine whether any such zone "has met the criteria established by the Committee," and recommend them to the respective governments, which "shall be responsible for seeking legislative approval for any amendments to the Agreement with respect to outward processing zones." The committee also is to "establish a maximum threshold for the value of the total input of the originating final good that may be added within the geographical area of the outward processing zone." Decisions of the committee would require "unified consent" (this arguably provides the U.S. side with veto power over any recommendation of the committee). The criteria to be met include but are not limited to "progress toward denuclearization of the Korean Peninsula; the impact of the outward processing zones on intra-Korean relations; and the environmental standards, labor standards and practices, wage practices and business and management practices prevailing in the outward processing zone, with due reference to the situation prevailing elsewhere in the local economy and the relevant international norms." The OPZ committee is to meet at least annually beginning a year after the agreement goes into effect.

Congress's Role

Annex 22-B gives Congress a role in deciding whether the products made in the KIC or other similar North Korean industrial parks would be included in the KORUS FTA. According to the terms of the agreement, the OPZ

Committee will pass its decisions to the South Korean and U.S. governments, which then would be responsible for "seeking legislative approval for any amendments" to the KORUS FTA. For years, neither the Bush nor Obama Administrations specified what form this "legislative approval" would take. In March 2011, the office of the United States Trade Representative (USTR) issued a statement that Congress "would need to pass, and the President would need to sign, a law to extend any KORUS tariff benefits to products made in Kaesong or any OPZ."[48]

Labor Standards and KIC Potentially Providing a Competitive Advantage

A question has arisen with respect to language in Annex 22-B pertaining to labor standards and practices in the KIC with due reference to the "situation prevailing elsewhere in the local economy and the relevant international norms." Is the local economy in this case that of the DPRK or that of South Korea, and can products from the KIC be produced under conditions contrary to International Labor Organization agreements that lay out basic international standards or worker rights yet still be recommended by the OPZ Committee to be included under the FTA?[49]

A further issue with respect to the KIC and the KORUS FTA is that if KIC products made with the low-cost North Korean labor are allowed to be treated as South Korean in origin under the proposed KORUS FTA, South Korean exporters would enjoy a large cost advantage over their counterparts in the United States.

Kaesong-Made Components and the KORUS FTA

Another issue raised by the KORUS FTA is whether intermediate products made in the KIC can enter the United States under the provisions of the FTA if they are incorporated into products that are manufactured in South Korea and that qualify as originating in South Korea. The same concern exists with respect to products made in China or elsewhere if they have North Korean inputs. Currently, discrete goods of North Korean origin may not be imported into the United States either directly or through third countries, without prior notification to and approval of the Office of Foreign Assets Control of the Department of the Treasury.[50]

If enacted, the KORUS FTA would likely have only a marginal impact on whether the United States imports goods that contain KIC-made components. The possibility of goods of South Korean origin with North Korean content exists now. KIC-made content could also increase due to the KORUS FTA increasing U.S. imports of South Korean manufactured goods above current levels. However, whether KIC-made components enter the United States is more likely to be determined by the future evolution of the KIC itself, rather than by the fate of the KORUS FTA. If the complex expands, and/or if KIC factories begin to make more components, then South Korean and other nations' companies could use them in manufacturing final products, which could then be exported to the United States and other countries.

The Control of Exports to Kaesong

The United States maintains restrictions on doing business with DPRK entities because of its designation as a state sponsor of international terrorism. All imports from North Korea into the United States require approval from the Office of Foreign Assets Control (OFAC), Department of the Treasury. The Department of Commerce licenses U.S. exports and re-exports, while Treasury grants general and/or specific licenses for financial transactions by U.S. persons with DPRK entities. The Department of Commerce requires a license for the export to North Korea of virtually all commodities, technology, and software, except for technology generally available to the public and gift parcels (not exceeding $400).[51] For instance, in FY2006, the U.S. Bureau of Industry and Security approved two items for export to the DPRK. They were glass (fiber optic) transmission items (5A99 1) worth $213,919 and software (5D992) for $3,600.[52] The transmission items were telecommunications equipment used by Korea Telecom in setting up the communications lines between the two Koreas and into the KIC.[53]

The South Korean government also maintains strict controls over exports to the DPRK. The restricted items include machinery and inspection equipment to produce metal and machines, electronics, optics, laser-related equipment, microorganism cultivating devices and chemical product facilities, and sophisticated high-technology equipment and materials. Even the latest versions of personal computers, commonly available in the South, are restricted and, if their export is approved, they have to be kept under lock and key in the KIC.[54] New high-technology monitoring systems, including tracking devices, are also being used for items with sensitive dual- use technology.

In the October 2007 summit between South Korean President Roh Moo-hyun and North Korean leader Kim Jong-il, the North agreed to improvements in how Kaesong operates, including swifter customs clearance for goods crossing its border, and better computer and cell-phone communications connections between Seoul and Kaesong factories. As mentioned above, the Lee government has made North Korea's implementation of these provisions preconditions for paying for the building of the dormitories that appear to be necessary for the KIC to undergo any significant expansion.

LONG-TERM GEOPOLITICAL AND ECONOMIC ISSUES

The Kaesong Industrial Complex sits at the hub of spreading concentric sets of economic and geopolitical interests and concerns. At its narrowest sense, the KIC is a business venture in which participants are seeking profits and business advantages. On the South Korean side, the KIC provides small and medium-sized companies with a manufacturing platform and opportunity to access low-cost labor without having to go overseas to establish subsidiaries or to outsource the assembly of their products to China or other markets. On the DPRK side, the KIC provides jobs for workers who can earn relatively higher wages without crossing their borders illegally or working under contract in labor-scarce countries such as those in the Russian Far East or in Middle Eastern countries.

At a somewhat wider set of interests, the KIC provides a channel for rapprochement between the DPRK and South Korea. Kaesong developed partly from South Korea's sunshine policy of economic engagement with the North. It can be viewed as a confidence-building measure between two countries whose hostility toward each other has lingered since the 1950-52 Korean War. As has been the case with the extensive economic interchange between China and Taiwan,[55] the KIC may provide a bridge for communication and a catalyst for cultural interaction, and it can create stakeholders in each other's economies with a shared interest in stability, liberalization, and increased communication across the DMZ.

At a still wider set of interests, the KIC may be the proverbial camel's nose under the tent in attempts to reform, liberalize, and modernize the North Korean economy. In neighboring China in 1978, foreign businesses were first allowed to operate in special economic zones. Now foreign invested businesses generate more than half of China's exports and imports. The Chinese speak of practicing socialism with Chinese characteristics and, indeed, many state-owned enterprises still encumber the Chinese economic system. The state-owned enterprises that are successful, however, operate much like privately owned enterprises, and one is hard pressed to find other significant differences between the Chinese brand of socialism and market capitalism. In May 2010, Kim Jong-il paid his fifth visit to China to visit special economic zones and to discuss issues. He also visited an industrial site.[56] Likewise, the KIC exposes average North Koreans to modern business methods and to the accouterments of Western industrial society.

According to the Economist Intelligence Unit, the decrepit North Korean economy has "three crying needs: deeper market reforms, greater openness, and above all, massive investment to modernize decrepit plant and infrastructure."[57] The KIC potentially addresses all three of these needs to a limited extent. However, reports from North Korea indicate that the economic reforms there currently are stalled—even being reversed. Unlike China's reforms, moreover, the initiative for the KIC came from abroad, is viewed with suspicion by many, and is an isolated case. Pyongyang, however, has renamed the Rajin-Sonbong region bordering China as Rason and is attempting to attract more Chinese investment there.[58] In sum, it is still too early to tell if Kaesong will succeed, much less have a large effect on the rest of the North Korean economy.

At a geopolitical level, Kaesong is one part of the standoff between the DPRK and the United States, China, South Korea, Japan, and Russia, over North Korea's nuclear weapons program. Under the rubric of the six-party talks lie a bundle of strategic issues, such as the ability of North Korea to finance its nuclear program, the need for humanitarian and energy aid, the stability of the Kim Jong-il regime, and the enforcement of various economic sanctions being applied to North Korea. A major goal of the United States in the six-party talks is to halt and verifiably dismantle North Korea's capability to produce nuclear fuel and nuclear bombs or to proliferate nuclear material or technology to potentially hostile countries or groups. The U.S. strategy to accomplish this is a combination of sticks (sanctions, diplomatic isolation, name calling) and carrots (promises of aid, diplomatic recognition, security guarantees) conveyed to North Korea through the six-party talks, bilateral meetings, and occasional media blasts. Under this strategy, there is little reason to provide the DPRK with any financial reward, even if it is to the benefit of South Korea, unless it shows significant progress in its commitments under the six-party talks. This is particularly the case if North Korea carries out attacks against South Korea.

The South Korean goals with respect to North Korea, however, not only include the denuclearization of the Korean peninsula but eventual reunification and reconstruction of the DPRK's economy. A major South Korean concern is the potential cost of reunification either in the form of a flood of economic emigrants to the South or in actual budgetary outlays to help rebuild the

North's civilian economy. The high cost to West Germany of the integration of East Germany after the fall of the Berlin Wall has provided little comfort to the policy makers in Seoul. The South Korean strategy, therefore, has tended to be longer on carrots (promises of food, fuel, and fertilizer) and shorter on sticks (sanctions) with a heavy reliance on engagement across the interactive spectrum and on diplomacy to resolve the issue. Even after the North Korean nuclear test in 2006, South Korea continued the KIC operations. It only halted its plans to call for new applicants to enter the KIC. Likewise, North Korea's provocations in 2010 did not result in the closing of the complex. Existing production facilities continued to manufacture and expand. Although ROK President Lee Myung-bak has said he will seek more reciprocity in Seoul's dealings with Pyongyang, and he has been somewhat vague about how he will treat the KIC, his statements and actions to date have been widely interpreted to mean that phase 1 of the complex, at a minimum, will continue operating. Undoubtedly, the KIC would be a centerpiece if Lee enacts his "Grand Bargain," under which South Korea would provide massive development assistance if North Korea dismantles its nuclear program.

For South Korea, not only does Kaesong provide entry into the decrepit DPRK economy, but it is a key factor in building up and reforming the economy in the North with an eye toward eventual reunification. Beijing's strategy before the return of Hong Kong in 1997 has been instructive to Seoul. A major reason that many of the first economic reforms in China occurred in nearby Guangdong Province, particularly just across the border from Hong Kong in Shenzhen city, was that Beijing tried to stem pressures to immigrate to Hong Kong by raising the standard of living and industrial development in the region abutting the returning territory. This strategy has been so successful that some immigration, particularly of Hong Kong retirees, has been going from Hong Kong to Guangdong Province and not the other way around. Likewise, Beijing has broadened ties with Taiwan through allowing cross-strait investments, travel, business visas, communication, and other business-based activities. In some sectors, particularly in the manufacture of computers and other electronic products, Taiwan and the east coast of China have become one integrated economy. Kaesong arguably could begin a similar process with North Korea.

South Korea also aims to become a hub of East Asia. In order to accomplish this, it would like to be connected to China, Russia, and to Europe via railways that pass through North Korea. As part of the KIC project, North and South Korea have reconnected a railroad line connecting the north and south and have conducted a test run on it. (A second line on the opposite side

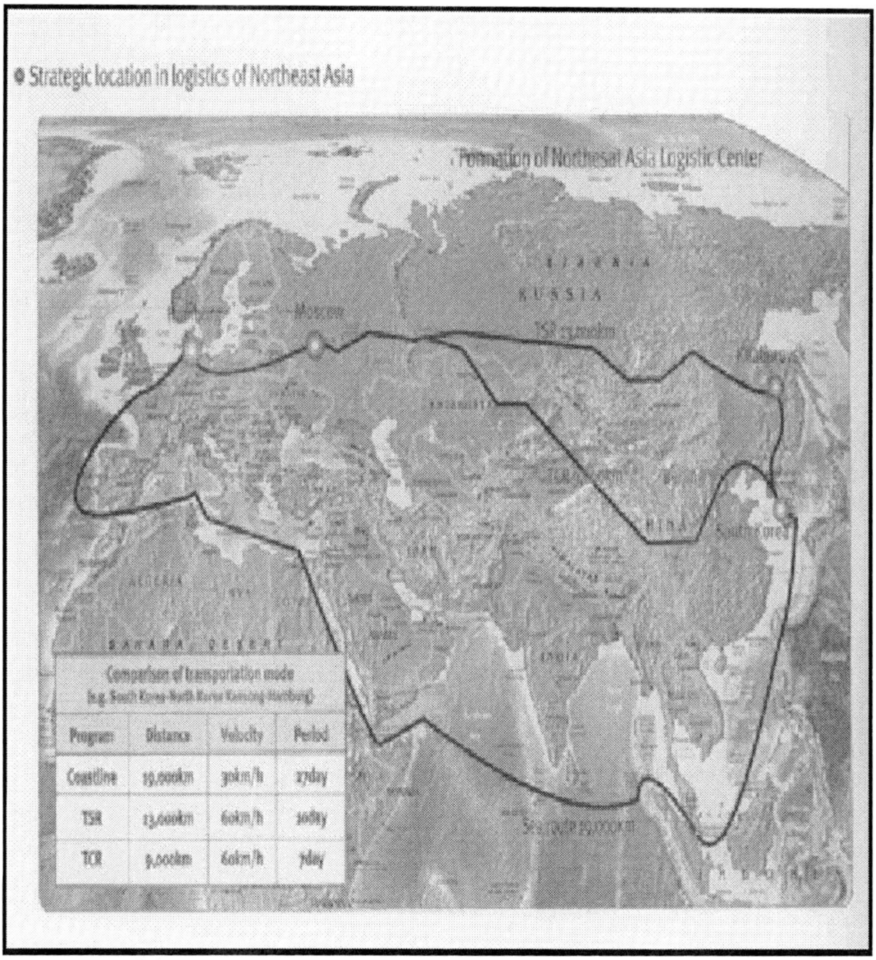

Source: Hyundai Asan.

Figure 2. Kaesong's Potential Logistical Role.

of the peninsula also was connected.) In terms of logistics, a shipment by rail from South Korea via Kaesong to Hamburg, Germany would take about 27 days by ship, 10 days via the Trans-Siberian Railway, and 7 days via the Trans-China Railway.[59] (See Figure 2.)

U.S. Interests and Policy Options

The three national interests of the United States that form the basis of all policy discussion are security, economic well-being, and value projection. These three national interests all play into consideration of the Kaesong Industrial Complex.

The main security concern for the United States is the location of the KIC in the DPRK. U.S. security concerns with respect to North Korea center on two major considerations: (1) the DPRK's nuclear program and (2) potential conflict across the DMZ separating North Korea and South Korea. The KIC has opposing effects upon these security considerations. On one hand, since income in any country is fungible, anything that increases revenue to the Pyongyang regime has the potential to contribute to the DPRK's military (including its missile and nuclear program). It is likely, however, that the DPRK's nuclear program has assured funding from the government. Also, given Kim Jong-il's "military first" policy, the North Korean military has top priority in the allocation of scarce economic resources. It also has call on certain economic activities and government subsidies for them. It is not clear how much, if any, income (over that used to pay for expenses related to Kaesong) for Pyongyang from the KIC currently is directed toward the DPRK military or nuclear program. Since the KIC land formerly was a military base that had to be vacated,[60] some arrangement may have been made to compensate the military for relinquishing a strategically important piece of ground. Even if the income from the KIC does not go directly into military purposes, it may bolster funds for civilian purposes that had been cut because of the budgetary demands of the military. The Kim regime, moreover, uses scarce foreign exchange to bolster the loyalty of its inner circle of elites who use it to buy imported luxury goods.

U.N. Security Council resolutions 1718 (adopted October 2006) and 1874 (adopted June 2009) explicitly prohibit any member state from providing funds that go to support North Korea's nuclear weapons program. Resolution 1718 states in Section 8(d) that all Member States shall, in accordance with their respective legal processes, ensure that any funds, financial assets or economic resources are prevented from being made available by their nationals or by any persons or entities within their territories, to or for the benefit of persons or entities engaged in or providing support for the DPRK's programs related to nuclear weapons, other weapons of mass destruction, and ballistic missile related programs.

As for tensions across the DMZ, the KIC already has played an important role in increasing the level of engagement between the DPRK and South Korea and in raising the priority of economic activity relative to security concerns. Even though the border between North Korea and South Korea is heavily guarded and crossings had been rare, the military on both sides have acquiesced to the daily traffic on the North-South highway to Kaesong and the re-connection of two railways across the DMZ (along with limited tourist visits and family reunions).

In terms of the second U.S. national interest of economic well-being, the KIC currently has little relevance, although it has some effect through U.S. trade and investment relations with South Korea. U.S. companies have no investments in Kaesong and U.S. trade with North Korea in 2009 was virtually non-existent. South Korea, however, is the seventh-largest trading partner of the United States, and the United States is South Korea's third-largest trading partner. If the six-party talks on the denuclearization of the Korean Peninsula were to re-start and progress far enough, the United States could re-establish diplomatic relations with the DPRK, lift economic sanctions, and eventually grant that country normal trade relations (most-favored nation) status. If so, trade with North Korea could be done on the same basis as trade with most other countries of the world. Absent that development, South Korea's request to treat products made in the KIC as South Korean in origin would seem to be the only way to bring the KIC into the set of industrial locations open to normal or preferential trade with the United States. Meanwhile, South Korean companies exporting KIC products likely will continue to avoid the U.S. market rather than face economic sanctions and high U.S. tariffs. This may give countries that include the KIC in their FTAs with South Korea (such as ASEAN and EFTA) a possible small diplomatic advantage over the United States in dealing with Seoul. Moreover, South Korea is likely to press the United States to change its KIC policy. This could be a source of future U.S.-ROK tension even if the KORUS FTA is passed.

The third U.S. national interest is projecting U.S. values such as a market-based economy, representative government, and nations adhering to world standards for working conditions, environmental regulation, and other humanitarian considerations. In this respect, the KIC potentially could play a significant role as a demonstration project to educate North Koreans on the workings of a market-based economy. The KIC provides an opportunity for businesses to operate in North Korea according to what may be higher labor and environmental standards than exist in the rest of the country and to educate North Korean middle managers on how such standards work.

Currently, the 40,000 North Koreans employed in the KIC are too few and the project too small to have a significant impact on the development of the North Korean middle class (a factor in the development of a more representative society), and the number of the elites in the DPRK with an economic interest in the complex probably is still relatively small. If the project continues to develop and the DPRK opens other free-trade zones, however, something akin to the economic reforms in China or the economic transformation that is now occurring in Vietnam[61] could occur in North Korea. This could weaken the hold by Pyongyang on the daily lives of citizens and bring the country more into the globalized world. Such economic liberalization also could reduce pressures on North Korea to engage in illicit trade in order to cover its trade deficit[62] and diminish the need for Pyongyang to saber rattle in order to divert attention from its domestic problems.

In the short run, however, increased revenues strengthen the regime's hand and make it less vulnerable to outside pressure. Also, spillover effects will depend on North Korea adding much more value to the production processes which it has yet to do. Finally, there is some question about the extent to which KIC is commercially viable, or whether incentives and supports given to South Korean firms are critical as opposed to marginal in their profit and loss calculations. Trade between the DPRK and South Korea tends to be government-based, in contrast to trade between China and North Korea. This may blunt the lessons learned by Pyongyang.

The United States currently has a mixed policy with respect to the KIC. Since South Korea is a close ally of the United States, Washington has been supportive of efforts by South Korea to engage the North in inter-Korean projects that benefit South Korea. On the other hand, the United States has been firm in predicating any economic or other concessions on actions by the DPRK to curtail or eliminate its nuclear program.

Major policy considerations and options for Congress, given the above U.S. interests, include the following:

- In considering whether or not to approve the KORUS FTA, Congress may express its support or non-support of the exclusion of the KIC from the FTA as negotiated. Congress may also specify the conditions under which the KIC can or can not be brought under the provisions of the proposed FTA. Congressional disapproval of the proposed KORUS FTA likely would have a large negative impact on prospects for the future of the KIC with respect to the United States.

- In the debate over the KORUS FTA, Congress may focus attention on labor and other conditions in the KIC and encourage reforms.
- If the KORUS FTA is approved, Congress may provide close oversight of the Committee on Outward Processing Zones.
- Since the United States already imposes a range of economic and financial sanctions on the DPRK, the United States could either tighten or loosen them. This could affect non-South Korean businesses in determining whether to invest in the KIC or to purchase products made there. The United States also could tighten (or loosen) U.S. controls on the export of dual-use technology items to the KIC.
- The United States could impose restrictions on or provide inducements to U.S. business activity in KIC.
- The U.S. government could encourage other countries (or groups of countries, such as the European Union) to (or not to) include the KIC in their respective FTAs with South Korea.
- If the DPRK takes the necessary steps to halt its nuclear program as outlined in the six-party talks, support (or oppose) measures leading toward normal trading relations status for the DPRK and the lifting of economic sanctions.
- The U.S. government could place restrictions on South Korean firms that do business in North Korea.

End Notes

[1] South Korean Ministry of Unification, as reported by U.S. Embassy Seoul Economic Section, *North Korea Economic Briefing*, January 21, 2011.

[2] South Korean Ministry of National Defense, "Investigation Result on the Sinking of ROKS 'Cheonan,'" May 20, 2010. The Joint Civilian-Military Investigation Group (JIG) included 25 South Koreans and 24 non-Korean civilian and military officials from the United States, Great Britain, Australia, and Sweden. North Korea has called the investigation's conclusion a "fabrication." Pyongyang Korean Central Broadcasting Station, "DPRK NDC Spokesman's Statement on ROK's Sunken Ship Investigation Results," May 20, 2010, as translated from the Korean by the Open Source Center.

[3] Office of the President of South Korea, "Special Address to the Nation by the President Lee Myung-bak," May 24, 2010.

[4] South Korean Ministry of Unification Press Release, "Announcement of Measures against North Korea," May 24, 2010. In March 2009, North Korea closed the North-South border for several days, leaving hundreds of South Korean workers unable to return home.

[5] "Press Statement by Spokesman for the Committee for the Peaceful Reunification of the Fatherland [CPRF]," Pyongyang Korean Central Television, May 25, 2010. Translated from the Korean by the Open Source Center, KPP20 100525104004.

[6] Stratfor.com, "Satellite Imagery: Tactical Details of the Korean Artillery Exchange," November 30, 2010.

Appendix A. List of Manufacturers in the Kaesong Industrial Complex

Table A-1. Manufacturers Operating in the Kaesong Industrial Complex As of February 2011

	Name of Company	Main Production Activity		Name of Company	Main Production Activity
1	Romanson (로만손)	Clock, Jewelry manufacturing	62	New Seoul Embroidery (새서울자수)	Clothing manufacturing
2	Aramode Watch Co.LTD (아라모드시계)	Watch manufacturing	63	HyupDong Textile Co., Ltd.(협동섬유)	Clothing manufacturing
3	Sin Han-guk Jungmil (신한국정밀)	Watch manufacturing	64	Dongwha (동화)	Thin-thread production and thread processing
4	Daepoong Watch Band (대풍시계밴드)	Watch manufacturing	65	한중실크유통	Burlap bag production
5	Pixies (픽시즈)	Jewelry, case for watch manufacturing	66	Best Friend (베스트프렌드)	Bags, rag doll production
6	Hyun Jin Precision Co (현진정밀공업사)	Watch manufacturing	67	Hanssem Corporation (한샘산업)	Kitchen utensils production
7	Lausanne Watch (로잔시계)	Watch manufacturing	68	SD&MALL (서도산업)	Apparel accessory manufacturing
8	N Gold Art.Co.LTD (엔골드아트)	Cubic zirconia processing	69	SDB (에스디비)	Mechanical parts production
9	Dongiljung Gongsa (동일정공사)	Watch manufacturing	70	Namkwang Engineering & Construction (남광토건)	Steel frame production
10	Samduck Corporation (삼덕통상)	Shoe & shoe parts manufacturing	71	Sunglim21 (성림정공)	Plastic goods production
11	Tae Sung Industry.Co (태성산업)	Cosmetic container manufacturing	72	Rok-Secz Garments Co.,LTD (록섹섬유)	Clothing manufacturing
12	Daewha Fuel Pump IND. LTD (대화연료펌프)	Auto parts manufacturing	73	Seil (세일)	Underwear materials manufacturing
13	Moon Chang Company (문창기업)	Clothing manufacturing	74	Changjin Apparel (창진어패럴)	Clothing manufacturing

	Name of Company	Main Production Activity		Name of Company	Main Production Activity
14	SJTECH Co. Ltd. (에스제이테크)	Electronic equipment production	75	Hongjin H.J (홍진에이치제이)	Motorcycle helmet manufacturing
15	Bucheon Industrial Co.LTD (부천공업)	Electronic parts production	76	Hong-ik Industry (홍익산업)	Food production
16	Jaeyoung Solutec (재영솔루텍)	Plastic goods production	77	YOUNG inner foam (영이너폼)	Underwear materials manufacturing
17	SHINWON Group Co.LTD (신원)	Clothing manufacturing	78	NINE (나인)	Underwear materials manufacturing
18	Sonoko Cuisineware (소노코쿠진웨어)	Kitchen utensils production	79	S & G (에스엔지)	Clothing manufacturing
19	Daekeon Corporation (대건실업)	Kitchen utensils production	80	SAE-A Trading Co.,LTD (세아상역)	Clothing manufacturing
20	JC Com Co. Ltd (제씨콤)	Communications device production	81	Al Dien Way (알디엔웨이)	Shoe manufacturing
21	Youngin Electronic Co.Ltd (용인전자)	Communications device, electronic parts production	82	Uni World (유니월드)	Auto parts manufacturing
22	HOSAN ACE Co.Ltd (호산에이스)	Mechanic, industrial-use refrigeration equipment production	83	Jahwa Electronics Co.,LTD (자화전자)	Electronic parts production
23	Migic LCD (매직엘시디)	Electronic parts production	84	J&J Trading Company (제이엔제이상사)	Auto parts manufacturing
24	TS Techonology Co.Ltd (티에스테크놀로지)	Semiconductor parts production	85	Myungjin Chemical (명진화학)	Electronic parts processing, Plating industry
25	Shinyoung Stain (신영스텐)	Kitchen utensils production	86	Hansfood (한식품)	Food production
26	JM P&P (조민포장)	Shopping bag, wrapper production	87	SM Techtex (에스엠테크텍스)	Clothing manufacturing
27	PYUNGAN Co.Ltd (평안)	Bedclothes production	88	Dongwoo Control Corporation (동우콘트롤)	Electronic parts production
28	ShinKwang Industry Co. Ltd (신광실업)	Underwear materials production	89	High-Low ENP (하이로이엔피)	Wrapper production
29	Han-guk Micro (한국마이크로)	Synthetic[chemical] fiber goods production	90	Prev (프레브)	Chemical plastic goods manufacturing
30	Peace Co.Ltd (평화유통)	Shoe production	91	Korea Electric Terminal Co.,LTD (한국단자공업)	Electronic parts production

Table A-1. (Continued)

	Name of Company	Main Production Activity		Name of Company	Main Production Activity
31	SUNGHWA Trading Co. Ltd (성화물산)	Apparel accessory production	92	Hankuk Chain Industrial Co.,LTD (한국체인)	Paper manufacturing, leather goods production
32	Mansun (만선)	Apparel production	93	Whain lenawoon (화인레나운)	Clothing and fur manufacturing
33	Goodpeople (좋은사람들)	Underwear materials production	94	Yoosung Industrial Co. (유성산업)	Leather bags, shoes manufacturing
34	Artrang (아트랑)	Apparel, bag production	95	Cuckoo Homesys Co.,,LTD (쿠쿠전자)	Home appliances manufacturing
35	Jeil Product (제일상품)	Underwear materials production	96	Daeil Textile Co., LTD (대일섬유)	Cotton fabrics manufacturing
36	Gin Gliders Inc (진글라이더)	Paraglide manufacturing	97	DKC Co., LTD (디케이씨)	Semiconductor carrier manufacturing
37	IS leports (일성레포츠)	Clothing manufacturing	98	Combase Inc (컴베이스)	Toner cartridge manufacturing
38	Evergreen (에버그린)	Clothing manufacturing	99	Doo Sung Tech (두성테크)	Electronic parts manufacturing
39	Teamsports (팀스포츠)	Clothing manufacturing	100	JMS Art Line (제이엠에스아트라인)	Textile manufacturing, sewing
40	Nine MODE.Co.Ltd (나인모드)	Clothing manufacturing	101	DMF (디엠에프)	Textile manufacturing, sewing
41	Two Line (투라인)	Clothing manufacturing	102	Jinwon Electronics (진원전자)	Chemical plastic goods manufacturing
42	Ergo Fashion (엘고패션)	Clothing manufacturing	103	C-net Connector (씨엔플러스)	Electric parts manufacturing
43	SM Bending (에스엠벤딩)	Clothing manufacturing	104	Seohan Textile (서한섬유)	Socks braid manufacturing
44	J. Fashion (제이패션)	Clothing manufacturing	105	Chon-il Trading Company (천일상사)	Textile manufacturing, sewing
45	A Jin Trading Co. (아진통상)	Clothing manufacturing	106	TaeKwang Industrial Company (태광산업)	Textile (Wool) manufacturing
46	Chic Bebe (쉬크베베)	Clothing manufacturing	107	Kyongdong Enterprise (경동흥업)	Socks and stocking manufacturing
47	Jinsung Industry CO., LTD (진성산업)	Clothing manufacturing	108	Baraque (바라크)	Shoe manufacturing
48	Dream F (드림에프)	Clothing manufacturing	109	Hans Industry (한스산업)	Shoe manufacturing

	Name of Company	Main Production Activity		Name of Company	Main Production Activity
49	Dong Woo Apparel (동우어패럴)	Clothing manufacturing	110	Poongyang Trading Company (풍양상사)	Textile manufacturing, sewing
50	Chang Dae Apparel (창대어패럴)	Clothing manufacturing	111	Bum Yang Glove Co.,LTD (범양글러브)	Textile manufacturing, sewing
51	SHC (신한물산)	Fishing net production	112	Dongyang Die Casting (동양다이캐스팅)	Metal assembling goods manufacturing
52	Y.S Korea Co.Ltd (와이에스코리아)	Clothing manufacturing	113	JINSUNG Tech (진성테크)	Plastic goods production
53	Geumdam (금담)	Clothing manufacturing	114	Amos Corporation (아모스)	Chemical goods manufacturing (Stationery)
54	S & T Sports (에스앤티스포츠)	Clothing manufacturing	115	Billy Willy (오오엔육육닷컴)	Clothing, Trade, e-commercial industry
55	Shinhan Mode (신한모드)	Clothing manufacturing	116	Seokchon Pottery (석촌도자기)	Ceramics manufacturing
56	Gwang-il (광일실업)	Clothing manufacturing	117	SAMAS (사마스전자)	Auto parts manufacturing
57	Sugn Lim Trading Company (성림상사)	Clothing manufacturing	118	KJC Socks Co. (아주양말)	Socks braid manufacturing
58	Woongpee Case (웅피케이스)	Clothing manufacturing	119	MAST (매스트)	Socks and stocking manufacturing
59	Shin's Design House (신즈디자인)	Clothing manufacturing	120	K2 Korea (케이투코리아)	Shoe manufacturing
60	Cheongsong Trade (청송무역)	Clothing manufacturing	121	BK Electronics Co.,LTD (비케이전자)	Electronic goods manufacturing
61	V.S&S Corp.Inc (뷔에세)	Clothing manufacturing	122	DSE (디에스이)	Electric lighting device manufacturing

Source: South Korean Ministry of Unification.

[7] "DPRK KPA Supreme Command's Communique on Artillery Gunfire Along Inter-Korean Border," Pyongyang Korean Central Broadcasting Station in Korean, November 23, 2010, translated by Open Source Center
KPP20101 123106004; "DPRK Commentary Says 23 Nov Clash Due to US, Civilian Casualties 'Very Regrettable'," Korean Central News Agency, November 27, 2010.

[8] "'Full Text' of ROK President Lee's 29 November 'Address to the Nation'," *Yonhap*, November 29, 2010. Lee said that for decades, South Korea had "tolerated provocations by the North time and again.... South Korea nonetheless endured these continual provocations because we entertained a slight hope that the North would change course someday.... At long last, we came to a realization ... that prolonged endurance and tolerance will spawn nothing but more serious provocations. If the North commits any additional provocations against the South, we will make sure that it pays a dear price without fail."

[9] These new firms were those who had been granted approval during the Roh Moo-hyun government.

[10] South Korean Ministry of Unification, *The Lee Myung-bak Administration's North Korea Policy*, May 2010, p. 45- 52.

[11] Under the Agreement Regarding Admission and Staying in the Kaesong Industrial Complex and Mt. Kumgang Special Tourism Zong (a.k.a. the Passage Agreement), the principle of compulsory repatriation of offenders was acknowledged by Pyongyang. This was important for South Korean businesses because under North Korean law, even crumbling a newspaper that displays Kim Jong-il's picture is considered a criminal act. (See Lim, Eul-chul. *Kaesong Industrial Complex, History, Pending Issues, and Outlook*, Seoul: Haenam Publishing Company, 2006, pp. 42-43.)

[12] Hyundai Asan. *Kaesong Industrial Park*, brochure. c. 2006. ROK. Ministry of Unification. Gaesong Industrial Complex: Frequently Asked Questions (May 21, 2006).

[13] Lim, Eul-chul. *Kaesong Industrial Complex*, op. cit., p. 172.

[14] South Korean Assembly Passes Bill on Inter-Korean Industrial Complex. Yonhap News Agency, April 27, 2007. Reported by BBC Monitoring Asia Pacific.

[15] Economist Intelligence Unit. South Korea Country Report. January 2008.

[16] Republic of Korea. Ministry of Unification. Gaeseong Industrial Complex Project—Status and Tasks, June 2005.

[17] Figures derived from statistics provided by ROK Ministry of Unification. See Table 3.

[18] ROK. Ministry of Unification. Gaesong Industrial Complex: Frequently Asked Questions (May 21, 2006).

[19] Lim, Eul-chul. *Kaesong Industrial Complex, History, Pending Issues, and Outlook*, Seoul: Haenam Publishing Company, 2006, pp. 68-69.

[20] Ibid., pp. 101-103.

[21] Ibid., pp. 108-126.

[22] Rights Body Criticizes South Korea Over Refugee Protection, Inter-Korean Complex. Yonhap News Agency, Seoul. Reported by BBC Monitoring Asia Pacific. London, January 12, 2007.

[23] Lefkowitz, Jay P. For a Few Dollars More, *Wall Street Journal*, January 10, 2007. p. A16.

[24] The DPRK has ratified no International Labor Organization conventions.

[25] Kaesong Industrial District Management Committee (KIDMAC), "Kaesong Industrial Complex," December 2009.

[26] Kaesong Industrial Complex Management Council. Survey of North Korean Workers from Fifteen Different Companies. February 2007. (Partial translation by the ROK Embassy in Washington, DC.)

[27] Ibid.

[28] ROK. Ministry of Unification. Gaesong Industrial Complex: Frequently Asked Questions (May 21, 2006).

[29] Hyundai Asan. *Kaesong Industrial Park*, brochure. c. 2006.

[30] South Korean Assembly Passes Bill on Inter-Korean Industrial Complex. Yonhap News Agency, April 27, 2007. Reported by BBC Monitoring Asia Pacific.

[31] ROK. Ministry of Unification. Gaesong Industrial Complex: Frequently Asked Questions (May 21, 2006).

[32] Ko, Gyoung-Bin. All the Salary Goes to the North Korean Workers at the Gaeseong Industrial Complex (GIC), January 31, 2007. Ministry of Unification document #uni4101.

[33] *North Korea Today*, No. 38, September 2006. Good Friends: Centre for Peace, Human rights and Refugees. September 27, 2006.

[34] Kaesong Industrial Complex Management Council. Survey of North Korean Workers from Fifteen Different Companies. February 2007. (Partial translation by the ROK Embassy in Washington, DC.)

[35] Lim, Eul-chul. *Kaesong Industrial Complex*, op. cit., p. 144.

[36] Ibid., p. 98ff.

[37] Ibid., p. 103.

[38] Communication from the Office of Korean Affairs, U.S. Department of State to the Congressional Research Service, June 7, 2007; 2011 communication with Ministry of Unification.

[39] Lim, Eul-chul. *Kaesong Industrial Complex, History, Pending Issues, and Outlook*, Seoul: Haenam Publishing Company, 2006, p. 144.

[40] Ibid., pp. 73-74.

[41] Ibid., p. 61.

[42] Merchandise FTA with Five ASEAN Countries to Take Effect Next Month. Yonhap News (Seoul), May 30, 2007.

[43] Channel News Asia, Singapore. *South Korea, Singapore Initial Free Trade Accord*, April 17, 2005. EFTA includes Iceland, Liechtenstein, Norway, and Switzerland. ROK, Ministry of Foreign Affairs and Trade. *Korea-European Free Trade Association (EFTA) FTA*, June 16, 2007.

[44] Lim, Eul-chul. *Kaesong Industrial Complex, History, Pending Issues, and Outlook*, Seoul: Haenam Publishing Company, 2006, p. 189.

[45] Article 15.2.1 of the EU-Korea Free Trade Agreement creates a Committee on Outward Processing Zones on the Korean Peninsula, which is described in Annex IV of the Protocol Concerning the Definition of 'Originating Products' and Methods of Administrative Co-Operation, http://trade

[46] For details, see CRS Report RL34330, *The Proposed U.S.-South Korea Free Trade Agreement (KORUS FTA): Provisions and Implications*, coordinated by William H. Cooper.

[47] Hyde Warns USTR to Keep Kaesong, Visas out of Korea FTA. *Inside US Trade*, July 21, 2006.

[48] March 2011 document issued by the Office Of The United States Trade Representative, "Outward Processing Zones, Kaesong, and the U.S.-Korea Trade Agreement Frequently Asked Questions"; Deputy United States Trade Representative reiterated this point in April 7, 2011 testimony before the House Ways and Means Trade Subcommittee.

[49] See Letter, Rep. Sander Levin, Chair of the House Ways and Means Subcommittee on Trade to Ambassador Susan Schwab, USTR. June 12, 2007.

[50] U.S. Treasury, Office of Foreign Assets Control. *North Korea: What You Need to Know About Sanctions.* c. 2007. See Title 31, Part 500, U.S. Code of Federal Regulations.

[51] U.S. Bureau of Industry and Security. Embargoed Countries and Entities (Section 746), Export Control Program Description and Licensing Policy. For information on U.S. export controls, see CRS Report RL3 1832, *The Export Administration Act: Evolution, Provisions, and Debate*, by Ian F. Fergusson.

[52] Bureau of Industry and Security, U.S. Department of Commerce, *Bureau of Industry and Security Annual Report, Fiscal Year 2006*. c. 2007, p. 93.

[53] The export license was approved by the U.S. Export Administration on November 16, 2005. (See Lim, Eul-chul. *Kaesong Industrial Complex, History, Pending Issues, and Outlook*, Seoul: Haenam Publishing Company, 2006, p. 206.)

[54] Ibid., p. 204.

[55] For a discussion of this issue, see CRS Report RL32882, *The Rise of China and Its Effect on Taiwan, Japan, and South Korea: U.S. Policy Choices*, by Dick K. Nanto and Emma Chanlett-Avery.

[56] See, for example, Wu Jiao, "Development is key during Kim's visit," *China Daily (Internet edition)*, May 5, 2010.

[57] The Economist Intelligence Unit. *Country Report, North Korea*, May 2007. p. 13.

[58] Scott Snyder, *Rajin-Sonbong: A Strategic Choice for China in Its Relations with Pyongyang*, China Brief Volume: 10 Issue: 7, The Jamestown Foundation, April 1, 2010.

[59] Hyundai Asan. *Kaesong Industrial Park*, brochure. c. 2006.

[60] Lim, Eul-chul. *Kaesong Industrial Complex, History, Pending Issues, and Outlook*, Seoul: Haenam Publishing Company, 2006. p. 37.

[61] See, for example, Bradsher, Keith, Vietnam's Roaring Economy Is Set for World Stage, *The New York Times,* October 25, 2006.

[62] See, for example, CRS Report RL33 885, *North Korean Crime-for-Profit Activities*, by Liana Sun Wyler and Dick K. Nanto.

INDEX

D

E

I

J

K

L

M

N

O

P

R

S

T

U

V

W